don't move, improve!

Room by room improvements to make the most of your home!

Contents	
First Impressions	11
Colour Choices	21
Kitchen	31
Lounge	43
Bedrooms	53
Bathrooms	67
New Additions	77
Garden	89

Text by Sara Porter.

This edition published in 2010 by L&K Designs.

PRINTED IN CHINA

Publishers Disclaimer

Whilst every effort has been made to ensure that the information contained is correct, the publisher cannot be held responsible for any errors and or omissions.

Don't move....

Budget

Unless you're in the fortunate position where money is no object, setting your budget should be your first point of call – it's no good coming up with great ideas if your budget won't stretch. So setting a realistic budget and sticking to it will be vital to your improvement plans.

Once you've an idea of what you want to improve and how, it's a good idea to set yourself up a budget sheet, noting down each different improvement and your projected budget. When writing your individual budgets, take into consideration any problems that could arise with particular improvements and give yourself a buffer-amount.

Keep a tally and watch that you're not going into the 'red'. If you've budgeted £300 for your bedroom and you end up spending £350 – then you'll need to mitigate your overspend by pulling back on other improvements, or waiting until you can comfortably complete them.

If you're considering extending or significantly altering parts of your home, do bear in mind the cost of architects and builders.

Basics

Once you've set your budget, think-out some basic considerations for your home improvement offensive.

Think practical first and prioritise, e.g. what needs repairing, what needs to be got rid of, what needs to be painted, etc. Once you've got those under your belt, you can think more creatively about what you'd like to create for your home.

What timescale do you intend to implement your changes within? Be realistic and take care not to put yourself under pressure. You may find that you need to make your improvements in stages.

Are your improvements long-term or short-term? For example, do you intend to paint your garden fence to make it look better in the short-term, until you can afford to replace it? There's no right or wrong to how you want to tackle it, but thinking of it in terms of longevity may help you with your decision making process.

Rather than plan every last detail by yourself; why not ask for a little help along the way? Whether you choose professional help or the help of trusted friends and family. It can be really beneficial to get other people's input, help and ideas.

What jobs can you do for yourself and which jobs will need professional help? Take an honest look at what needs to be done and your personal limitations; whether it be time, ability or practicality – if it's going to be too much to do yourself and you have the means, it might well be a worthwhile investment.

Shop Around

Home improvement can be an expensive business, but chances are that if you're canny and apply a bit of shopping know-how you can find essential deals and discounts that will make your budget go much further than you might have thought possible.

Before you start purchasing, check out your local hardware stores and the larger home improvement stores for their latest offers. With more and more people deciding to improve their homes, the competition between stores is far fiercer than you realise – so take advantage of it! The Internet is a fast and easy way to do your research, but also keep your eye open for TV advertisements and promotional leaflets.

Ideas Board

Make an ideas-board, organiser or scrapbook; this way you can keep all your cuttings, printings, swatches, ideas and inspirations for your improvements in one easily accessible place.

Legalities

Make sure that you check into laws and regulations pertaining to your property and home improvements/building works before you begin any new projects. You may think that erecting a cute little picket-fence to nicely round off your front garden isn't an issue – but your local council and neighbours might feel differently.

Think Practicalities

Think over practicalities carefully, for example…if you have limited and light 'traffic' shuffling to and from the entrance to your home, then you are less likely to need to consider significant practical issues.

However, if your entrance is regularly besieged by kids, dogs, bicycles, mucky boots, (of the adult and child variety!), muddy footballs, wet school gear and soggy sports bags, etc… then practicalities will need to feature as part of your planning.

Of course, no-one can tell you that cream carpets, with matching fabrics and walls can't be what you aspire to – if that's what you really want, then go for it! Just be prepared for lots of spot-cleaning and maybe even creating a back-door entrance for your family!

So before you begin, take some time out and think about what you want and whether your ideas are practicable for your home. Here are a few suggestions to think over :-

*   What sort of lifestyle to you and you family live – and what kind of home does that lifestyle need… e.g. a calm, ordered, tidy or cosy home?

*   Which room does everybody naturally gravitate to?

*   Are you a bit of a social butterfly? If so, are you likely to hold dinner parties or other social events at your home?

*   If you have children, do they have hobbies? What space do you need to accommodate their activities?

*   Do you need space in the house for peace and quiet, away from the hubbub of the rest of the house?

Schedule

To keep yourself on track, it's a good idea to set a realistic schedule for your improvements. It doesn't have to be so rigid that you find yourself having to crack an imaginary whip to make yourself complete tasks – but something that will keep you focused and inspired. It's also a good idea to know what time of day your energy levels peak – it's no good having to get up at the crack of dawn if you resemble something more like the 'living-dead' at that time! You'll just be grumpy and unproductive. Pick your best time of day and start from there.

Be Committed

Before beginning any of your home improvements, make sure that you are 100% committed to getting it done. If any of your ideas are half-hearted or a bit wishy-washy, then put them off until you're sure about what you want – you don't want to give yourself a reason to not finish projects. Of course, that doesn't mean that you won't take on any projects that you end up wanting to change, because that's the nature of you getting creative with your house – but you're less likely to be in that position if you feel that you're committed to your ideas from the outset.

Extensions & Conversions

There are many ways for you to improve your home, one popular way being to add space by building an extension, or converting an existing or non-living area. Of course, this is a more expensive option, but it may be that by gaining an extra room or creating a bigger space you'll not only be making an important improvement, but also an investment in your home.

Think Carefully

One thing to remember about such radical improvements is to carefully consider the style and proportions of your house; your extension might look great in your minds-eye but in reality it may end up being an eyesore. It's also worth considering the flow of your house, in terms of space, noise and traffic. For example, opening up your stairway into the living room may seem like a great plan, but when you can then hear the thump-thumping of your teenagers latest rock band over the television, you may wish you'd not bothered!

First Steps

If you're seriously considering an extension or conversion, then you'll need to follow a few necessary steps:-

Obtain planning permission from your local authority. If you don't and you go ahead regardless, you could well face being in the position of being told to undo the work that you've had done.

Find an architect to discuss and draw-up your ideas. They will be able to advise you and throw up any difficulties that they can foresee. Your local authority is likely to want a copy of official plans before you're given permission anyway – so a good architect is a must.

Find a reputable builder – although, that's sometimes easier said than done. Whatever you do, don't pick the first name that you find in the local directory or on the Internet. The best way to find a good builder is to take a direct recommendation from a friend or relative.

If that's not possible then look to the Federation of Master Builders and pick three builders to come and supply quotes. Ask for testimonials from former customers, along with their contact details – a good builder will expect you to check them out, so don't feel awkward asking.

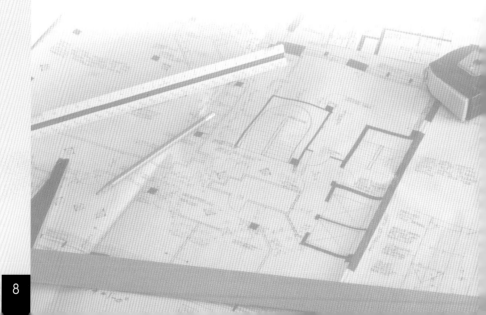

Popular Extensions & Conversions

Loft Conversions: a wonderful way to achieve greater living space, without it altering the external look of your home. Some proper thought about ladder/stair access will be needed though.

Ground Floor Extensions: used to create a wide range of extra space requirements; office space, playroom, bigger kitchens, dining rooms, lounges, etc.

Basements: an expensive way to extend your property than the more traditional sideways or upward extensions, but worth it in terms of space if you can do it.

Garages: the majority of garages these days are too small to house all but the smallest of cars, so end up being extra storage space – but if directly next to the house, they can make great extensions into bedrooms, playrooms, offices, etc. If your garage is further up the garden, costs will be far greater and it's better to talk to an estate agent, if adding value to your property is part of your decision making process.

Conservatories: a very popular and probably the most inexpensive way of adding extra living space to your home. Although lovely in the warmer months, make sure that you've blinds and heating for the winter months to make it an all-year-round space.

Be Prepared!

Make no mistake, taking on an extension or conversion will cause some chaos – to greater or lesser degrees. So think through your timing and how you're going to accommodate the work and resultant changes. Once you've started, don't lose sight of the end goal and remember that there's an end point at which you'll reap the benefits. After all, it was your choice to make the changes, so keep your sense of humour about it!

First Impressions

First impressions count...

Window Boxes
Decorative window boxes are a delightful addition to any home. A bright and colourful way to improve the outside of your house, you have a wide variety of choice in terms of flowers – choices that can be changed with each season. Paint the colour of your window box to match the outside of your window; or if you really want to make a statement, paint it in a vivid colour to match your colourful flower choices!

Hedge Your Bets
Is the route to the entrance of your house a little lacking in greenery? Perhaps your front pathway could benefit from a more established boundary? If so, then a hedge just might be the eco-friendly way to go – as well as making an aesthetic improvement, you'll also be providing a home for wildlife and friendly insects.

Alternatively, if you have an existing hedge, you may want to give it a bit of a makeover! Shape it into an elaborate entrance/boundary to your house. Flowering hedges will also add an extra edge, adorning blooms that will be attractive to look at for both you and your neighbours.

Hanging Baskets
Hanging baskets can quickly brighten up the dullest doorway and add a welcome sparkle to any bare patio or porch. If you opt for these beautiful floral additions, be aware that they are quite labour intensive, needing lots of water, feeding and dead-heading.

Wall Climbers
A really natural and stunning way to improve your bare, brick walls is to introduce climbing plants or erect trellises adorned with flowers. Pruning and proper care will be key to their success and beauty - and also as an aid to ensure that they don't run wild!

Take the edge off the outside corners of your house by planting shrubs or by erecting trellises with climbers or vines. This is considered good practice from a feng shui perspective.

Pathway/Driveway & Steps

The entrance to your house should be welcoming – it's the walkway to your home, so it's there to bring the people that you know and love into your domain.

Make sure that weeds, leaves, moss and unwanted grassy areas are kept on top of. Prevent weeds from infiltrating your walkways by sprinkling rock salt over the area in spring. The salt will soak into the ground area in between and kill off any weeds that would be ready to make their appearance during growing season.

Level any uneven paves and replace any cracked, broken or loose steps, so that they don't create a hazard on the walk up to your home – and they'll look better too.

Make sure that the pathway doesn't flood or become a mud-bath when it rains. Apart from it being an annoyance to your guests – you'll be the ones treading muck into your house!

If you want to give the pathway and steps to your house a colourful facelift, think about resurfacing it by laying a red brick veneer.

If your pathway leads straight up to your front door, you might want to consider re-shaping it to incorporate slight curves, making it appear a little 'gentler' and aesthetically more interesting.

Light up the entrance to your house in the evenings by planting solar-powered lights along the side of the pathway.

With their own natural source of power, you won't need to worry about them being high maintenance or a drain on energy – and they look delightful.

Letter/Post Box

Is your letterbox looking a little lack-lustre? Give it a coat of paint to freshen and brighten it up – or if it's a little on the unsalvageable side, then why not invest in a new one? They don't cost the earth and you'll be surprised at what a difference it will make to your door. If you'd like to keep your post separate to your front hallway - perhaps to keep it clutter-free or to stop over-enthusiastic dogs from having a mid-morning brunch of bank statements… then how about erecting a lockable post-box on the outside of your house? You can either fix them to an outside wall, or have them free standing. With a rise in popularity, there are some great designs out there, try www.simplypostboxes.co.uk as a source of inspiration.

Fencing

Give old, grey fencing a facelift with a coat of varnish or outdoor paint. Just that one aesthetic change can make it look like a different fence – as well as giving your fence a layer of protection against the elements, preserving it for longer.

Entwine your fencing with beautiful, fragrant flowers by planting climbers alongside. But make sure that they don't overwhelm the fence in terms of weight and growth.

If you don't have fencing, your home may benefit from the introduction of some attractive-looking fencing. You don't have to erect anything large or intimidating, just something that will define your boundaries and create a feeling of space and privacy.

Garages

If your house is designed with the garage being located near to, or visible from the entrance to your house, then it's appearance is going to be part of what you and your visitors see as a first impression.

It's possibly a building that you don't consider to be part of your home, but despite it's purely functional part in your life, it still requires your attention in terms of how it looks. No good having a stunning outer image to the main house and Garden, when your garage still has the original paint on it from 15 years ago!

Painting it as part of your improvements will make a world of difference – just be aware of not falling into the trap of painting it a bright colour that detracts attention away from the front of your home. Your front door should be your focal point, not the garage door!

Front Gate

Front gates provide us with a defined boundary between our homes and the outside world. Whether they are small wooden gates or large, wrought iron gates – they give us a sense of security, knowing that once we walk through them we are home.

Look at your gates, what do they say? Do they say, "Come in…you're welcome", or do they say, "Keep out…unless you're invited"? There's no right or wrong here, what matters is what YOU want them to say. You may have very good reason to give off a message of not wanting uninvited callers – as equally, you may be happy for the world to knock on your door. Whatever your message, your front gates will be an integral part of the first impressions that you communicate to the world.

For existing gates, there a lots of ways that you can improve them; give them lick of paint, stain and waterproof them, coat them with anti-rusting products, adorn them with a, "Welcome" (or "Keep Out"), sign… or just simply give them a good clean!

Foundations

If your house is surrounded by unattractive foundations, disguise them with ground plants. Plant a mixture, e.g. all year-round greenery, bulbs, perennials, shrubs, etc. Just ensure you choose plants whose roots will not become invasive to the foundations.

Front Doors

As the key symbol of 'welcome' to our homes, our front door is the one place that we pass in and out of on a daily basis and that acts as the primary point of access to our inner worlds.

By simply freshening up the door with a coat of paint, or changing the colour, you can transform the appearance of your home dramatically. If you're thinking of a new colour, think about any decorations or items that you want to have directly outside your door – for instance, if you like to hang evergreen wreaths on the door, or hanging baskets to the side of the door, pick a colour that will enhance your decorations not hide them.

When choosing your paint ensure that you select a good quality exterior paint, that will withstand the elements. And if you've not got the time to paint the rest of the outside of your house, giving special attention to your front door will attract your eyes away from old, tired paint to bright, clean new paint!

Other easy ways to 'dress-up' your front door include adding an attractive-looking door knob/handle, positioning an ornamental light fixture beside the door, (preferably one that has an energy-saving sensor), hanging evergreen wreaths on the door, adorning the wall beside the door with a hanging basket or adding numbers or the name of your house with a decorative plaque.

Exterior Paint Colours

When you're considering your colour palette for painting the outside of your house, think about whether the colours you like will match the style and period of your house. You might love light, pastel colours but they could look hideous on the outside of your Victorian-era built home.

If you're feeling a little lost in terms of inspiration, have a look around at houses in your area and see what sort of colour schemes and styles appeal to you.

Take into consideration the fact that deep, rich and bright colours will fade on the outside, so just bear in mind that they will be more labour intensive in terms of maintenance.

Windows

Windows are the eyes of our home, creating a big impact on those first impressions. Windows can really make a difference to how our house looks, from an internal and external perspective.

Giving the woodwork a lick of fresh paint and the glass a really good clean, (inside and out!), can make the world of difference to them.

If your windows are in dire need of replacing, then see them as an important investment – you could be losing vital energy from your home, regardless of the aesthetics. When shopping for your replacement windows, think carefully about your new windows being appropriately sized and styled to match the style and 'period' of your home. There are plenty of suppliers out there – and some a little on the unscrupulous side, so do your homework before you commit to a sale and look into reviews and testimonials of previous customers.

If the size and style of your house will accommodate it, then why not incorporate some stained glass into your home? They look stunning with the sun shining through them, creating beautiful tones of light and warmth inside your home; as well as looking striking from the outside.

Hallway/Entrance Area

Regardless of whether you have a large entrance hallway or a few paces before you move into the main part of the house, your hallway is the gateway to your home.

As the focal point of entry, this is an important place in making those internal first impressions count. It provides visitors with an insight into how you and your family live and introduces them to the rest of your house. This is also the part of the house that will greet you when you come home at the end of each day – so you want it to be welcoming to you too.

Pictures & Artwork

Inject the entrance to your house with a real insight to your personality by adding well-chosen decoration for the walls. It can be a favourite painting(s), treasured family photos, crafted tapestry, wall décor from your holidays/travels or other items that will reflect your individuality. Your hallway can also be home to interesting sculptures. Use lighting to highlight your choices and to give your pieces the prime of place in your hallway.

Wind Chimes

Add a welcoming tinkle by positioning a wind chime by your front door. Kids love them and they're a pleasant way of telling you that someone's arrived!

Freshen up with Paint

A fresh coat of paint will always make a difference to any room and as hallways experience more traffic than most other rooms in the house, maintaining the walls will be an important factor in home improvements. It's usually best to select a heavy-duty, durable paint for hallways – something that is easy to wipe and chip-resistant.

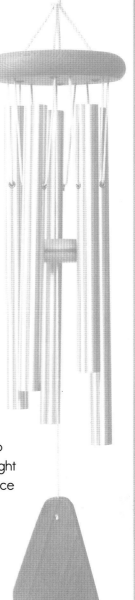

Colour Scheme

Choosing your colour scheme for your entrance hall may well depend on whether you have children and/or pets. If you've none of either, then light, calm tones will create a feeling of relaxation, (as well as a polite message of "Take your shoes off please!"). If, on the other hand, you have children and/or pets, then it's probably best to think practically about colours. That said, it doesn't mean that you're out of the 'beige-market' – it's just probably better to go for slightly darker, warmer tones.

Furnish with Pride!

If you have the space, place a well-chosen furnishing in your hallway, something that is both aesthetically pleasing as a focal point and functional. For instance, an attractive bureau-style piece of furniture which looks beautiful, but that can also be used for storage for outdoor items such as hats, scarves, gloves, etc. Or, a stylish table that can house pictures, flowers, lamps or seasonal displays.

Go Floral

Simple but always effective, fresh flowers are an eye-catching addition to any room – and in the entrance to your home, it's a welcoming sight for all family members to come in to. So whether you go for white, elegant lilies, multi-coloured blooms or both – flowers will bring beauty and fragrance into those vital first impressions.

Brighten & Lighten

Good lighting is essential in setting the tone and warmth of your home. If your hallway struggles for light then choose light, fresh washable colours for your walls – if practicalities allow. If there's a window leading into the hallway, don't obscure the light coming through. A beautiful light can be used as the centerpiece of your hallway. If space is an issue, avoid pendant lighting as this will have the effect of bringing the ceiling down and making the space feel smaller; use down-lighters instead. If you want to create a dramatic effect, use up/down lighting, positioning them to accentuate chosen points of your hallway. If you prefer more subtle lighting, use low wattage bulbs or stylish lamps that will light up selected areas of your hallway.

Mirror, Mirror...

As well as creating extra light in hallways, mirrors can provide really beautiful decoration for hallways and stairwells. A large, long mirror can make a very narrow hall seem wider and bigger; as well as reflecting brilliant light back into the area. It's also an extra mirror in the house for those last minute touches before you leave the house!

Remove the Clutter!

Usually consisting of a mind-numbing mixture of everyone's bits and pieces, hallways have a way of attracting clutter like no other part of the house! So, a very simple part of your home improvement is to remove the clutter! Be dynamic – if it's not supposed to be there, move them to it's proper home. And make sure that you get those responsible for leaving items there to move them; otherwise you'll be fighting a losing battle.

Storage

There will inevitably be items in your hallway that you might not want to see, but that practically belong there, such as; shoes, umbrellas, coats, keys, etc. To give you a sense of immediate improvement, investigate suitable forms of storage. Think about shoe racks/cabinets, umbrella stands, coathooks/stands, key hooks, shelving, baskets, ottomans, etc. If you've a stairwell that leads into your hallway, then you might have unused areas underneath that could be converted into suitable storage spaces.

Stairway

Your stairway, (if you have one), may run into your hallway area; making it an important focal point to the entrance of your house. Make it look extra-special and inject more of your personality into it by placing colourful pictures, photos or other artwork on the wall running up the side. If your landing at the top of the stairs has enough space, adorn it with a piece an ornate piece of furniture, such as an attractive table or chair.

Flooring

Depending on your practical needs, the flooring in your hallway will communicate more of who you and your family are. Thick, luxurious carpets greeting you at the front door are a reasonably good indication of a comfortable and cosy home – but be ready to take your shoes off! If adding a carpet appeals to you as a home improvement, then be sure to seal your carpet with a quality protective spray once it's laid. For existing carpets, why not invest in renting a carpet cleaner for a good old-spot of spring-cleaning!

Hard, durable surfaces are good for heavy traffic, being easy to clean and less at risk of damage. However, they can make hallways look quite stark and they tend to be a magnet for dust and muck in the corners – as well as being pretty noisy. One way to soften and warm up a hallway with a hard floor is to add a runner or rug, this will provide the hard areas for mucky feet top tread and then soft-luxury on carpet for your feet once your shoes are off!

Make it Welcoming

If you've room, perhaps place a chair or double-seat against a wall in your hallway – it says, "Come in and take a pew", allowing your visitors to rest themselves for a minute when they come in, or giving them somewhere welcome to sit and take off their shoes.

Colour Choices

Colour Choices

Colour Your Home Happy!

No doubt you won't have escaped the variety of home improvement programmes, telling us to go with safe neutrals, such as creams and beiges in order to create a blank canvas for prospective buyers… or to keep your home 'in vogue'. But, Don't Move, Improve, isn't an exercise in doing what the experts tell you – it's about really claiming your house as your own and improving it in a way that makes you and your family happy.

That's not to say that neutrals are a 'no, no' – because if you enjoy having those clean, easy to coordinate tones, then absolutely go with what you love and feel comfortable with. But if you'd like to convert your home into something a bit more daring and colourful, something that you feel reflects yours and your family's personalities…then go for it! You're not moving, you're improving!

Inspiration

Creative Input

If the thought of re-decorating sparks off feelings of fear and anxiety, then why not ask for some assistance? We're not all blessed with the imaginative flair that we'd like, so if you have a friend or family member whose style you admire – then why not ask for their creative input and help in your decision making process? That way you can gleam different creative styles and ideas, as well as feeling supported.

Involve the family

Get together with all the members of your family and 'brain-storm' ideas for each area of the house that you want to decorate. You're not stuck with the dilemma of having to make your house 'buyer-friendly' – so you can really delve into all the possibilities and have fun discovering what's right for you as a family. If you have children, take on board their likes and dislikes and allow them to have some control over their own space. If they want to have dark, deep-blue walls with star and moon stencils, then why not? It's their room! More daring colours are easily painted over when the novelty inevitably wears off as your children grow-up. And you can cunningly use it as a little bit of leverage, i.e. they get the colours that they want, as long as they promise to keep their rooms tidy!

Resources

If you're struggling for ideas get some inspiration from magazines, newspapers, books, TV, etc. Fabric shops are a good resource for getting a grounded professional opinion on what colour groups go together well – and you can see them laid out in front of you in a contained space.

Just be aware that you don't have to conform to stereotypical ideas of how your house 'should' look. Use these resources as inspiration, rather than an absolute template of what you need to do – and take your time.

Keep an Open Mind

Whatever your preferred choice of colour or decorating style, the most important thing is to keep an open mind in terms of exploring creative and innovative possibilities where improving your home is concerned. Don't shut yourself down with fear about being a bit more daring – what's the worst thing that could happen? Basically, you'll just have to paint over it! It might be a pain, but it's not the end of the world.

What Makes You Happy?

No matter what influences you pick up along the way, in the end the most important aspect to improving your home is choosing colours that make you feel happy and that bring feelings of contentment to your home.

It's your life and your home, so you choose what you want to surround yourself with. Your house doesn't have to look like a showroom, (unless you want it to, of course) – as long as it meets your ideal.

Colour Decorating Tips

Step-by-Step
If you're a bit of a 'newbie' in terms of coordinating colours using large areas, then you might not want to dive straight into a deep maroon coloured living room! Start by perhaps stepping up a shade or two, with a colour tone that you're familiar with and paint one wall. Don't go on your immediate reaction, live with it for a few days and see how you feel.

Colour Freedom!
Popular interior design advice posits that it's necessary to have each of the rooms in your house to follow a similar colour scheme, flowing the colours from room to room… forget THAT! This is about you and your home – these are your choices. So, if you want to have an earthy, rustic style living room with lots of warmth and colour – and then a fresh, minimalist-style kitchen, then that's entirely up to you! Don't get too hung up on what the experts tell you – this is YOUR home!

Light & Space
When you're deciding your colour schemes, in order to optimise the feeling of space in each room, take into account the size of the room and the lighting – both natural daylight and artificial indoor lighting. Light colours are usually better in darker, smaller spaces, whereas bolder tones are better suited to larger, lighter areas.

Climate & Tones
As well as thinking about the size and lighting in a room, think about the 'climate' you want the room to imbue, e.g. does the room suit cool, fresh colours or deep, warm, cozy tones.

Furniture & Features
Use items that you already own for further inspiration, maybe you have a favourite rug, or furniture throw that you'd like to incorporate into your choice of tones and colours. Take into account what furniture and features are going to be in each room, as well as the flooring and woodwork. Incorporating these accent colours and tones will be integral in helping you to determine your colour options.

Try Out Samples

Before committing to colours, it's a good idea to buy sample pots and try them out first. The colours in the brochures and on the outside of the tins will look different on your walls, plus they will also change according to what type of light is shining on them, e.g. daylight, halogen lamps, bulbs, etc. So, make sure that you keep tabs on the changes of colours at different times of the day.

Preparation is Key

Filling, sanding and smoothing walls and woodwork before painting them makes your painting efforts look far more effective and professional.

Wallpaper – Likes & Dislikes

If you're choosing wallpaper as part of your decorating plans, note down your likes and dislikes before setting out, e.g. do you love florals and stripes? Or do prefer bold patterns and large prints?

Colour Choices

A World of Colours

We can't under estimate the power of colour in our lives. Just think about how we feel when we look out the window and the sun is shining and the sky is stunning blue… or when see the radiant beauty of a red and gold sunset… or a black sky filled with the promise of a spectacular storm.

The colours that we dress in give important non-verbal messages - a brightly coloured outfit against a charcoal coloured suit will speak their own words to those around us.

Decorating your home can be seen as an extension of how you feel about your life, each individual room reflecting a part of your inner world. So, choosing your colour schemes informed by what you love, and what you feel is good for you, will make your decision making process much easier. Here are some pointers on some popular colours and their meanings: -

Beige

A popular neutral, beige is a versatile colour. Calm and relaxing, beige comes in a variety of different tones and shades.

The mixture of cool white and warm, earthy browns makes beige an easy colour to coordinate and to contrast with darker, stronger colours.

Alternatively, use it on it's own as a simplistic and classic backdrop.

Blue

Blue conjures up the calm of the ocean and the visual beauty of the sky, whether it be the stunning, bright blue of a sunny, cloudless sky or the more mysterious, deeper blue of the evening twilight. Blue as an energy has a cool, calm and soothing vibration – perfect for the home.

Blue can create a light and peaceful environment, but be careful not to make your room too cold – perhaps add items which will provide a little warmth. Darker blues, combined with lighter shades will create a classic look.

Brown

The literal colour of earth; brown is natural, down-to-earth, warm, dependable, simple and wholesome. Ranging from light neutral tones to deep, reddish autumnal browns the colour schemes that can comfortably accommodate brown bring a sense of stability and comfort.

Browns can be used in their lighter shades of beige, tan and taupe with either creams or deeper colours of brown. Darker browns are perfect for reds, yellows and even certain shades of blue.

Green

Green is the colour of nature and life; without life's 'greenery' we would not be able to exist. Olive green, fresh springtime green, shamrock green, lime green, forest green, moss green – the options for green in your house are plentiful. Green's energy represents natural balance and personal growth; its presence in your colour scheme will promote a restful and harmonious environment.

Green is available in such a wide range of shades that make it an incredibly versatile colour to use.

Use darker and lighter shades of green together to create a natural feel.

Grey

Grey is the new beige! Grey is the ultimate neutral colour and with it comes a huge range of versatility. Grey energy imparts dependability, practicality and stability.

Using grey as a room colour may seem a little on the formal side, but give it chance. Grey has a non-threatening vibration, which against stronger, more vibrant colours brings a sense of harmony and balance. Use light grey instead of white and dark, charcoal grey instead of black. Grey with a silver, metallic tone can bring an exciting energy to a room.

Ivory

Softer, warmer and more elegant than white, ivory is a popular backdrop for accommodating practically any colour scheme. Ivory is a calm, relaxed colour; giving rise to a feeling of purity and peacefulness.

Using ivory will give you the clean lines of white, without it being stark or clinical. If you want to go for an understated colour scheme, ivory can be used either on it's own or alongside other colours to create contrast.

Orange

An incredibly powerful and flamboyant colour, orange is associated with warmth, energy and healing. Just think of the fruit, it's natural source of vitamin C and how it taps into our sense of health and wellbeing. Whether you choose the softer, peachy shades, the warm glow of the sun's rays, or the burnt, autumnal tones of orange – this colour gives a versatile and welcoming colour to our homes.

Used as an accent or in wider coverage, orange is a warm and cosy colour, providing a less powerful sense of warmth to a room than daring red.

Pink

Traditionally thought of as being a 'feminine' colour, pink comes in a myriad of different shades and tints...such as bubblegum, cotton candy, pastel, magenta, baby, cerise, hot and rose. Pink's energy is relaxing, calming, caring and ever associated with love and romance.

Different shades of pink can be used together; darker pinks can be used to add depth to lighter shades; alongside burgundy and purples for even greater intensity.

Purple

Purple is associated with royalty and spirituality, in almost equal doses. Combining the coolness of blue and the heat of red, purple is a striking colour combination. As an energy purple is peaceful, spiritual and mysterious.

Used in a variety of shades, which can combine more of a red tone or blue tone, to create warmer or cooler looks, purple has amazing versatility.

If you're going for a stronger, deeper purple, keep in mind that too much can be overwhelming, but just the right amount will create a stunning effect.

Mixing it with lighter shades of purple or subtle pinks will work to mitigate too much depth. Lighter more gentle tones of purple, such as lavender, lilac and violet, which create a more graceful and romantic feel to a room.

Red

Classically the warmest colour – gregarious, passionate, lively, vivacious, animated and confident; red is the colour of energy and life. Red is a colour that can enthuse, vitalise and comfort those around it. On the negative side it can also be seen as the colour of anger and stirred emotions, i.e. "seeing red", or as an alert to danger.

Red is an incredibly personal colour and most of us are split into two definitive camps, of either 'love it' or 'hate it'. Red's dominating tone will ensure that it captures attention – so if you've never used it before, you might want to start with using it as an accent colour. But if you're going for purposely looking for a bold statement, then red could be your colour.

Yellow

Yellow is associated with happiness, joy and creativity…think bright sunshine, buttercups, spring chicks, daffodils…the Yellow-Brick-Road even! A cheerful and welcoming colour, rooms can be transformed instantly with it's pure clarity and glow. Shades will range from pastel lemons through to bright, golden yellows.

Yellow is perfect as an accent to compliment other warm or earthy colours, or if you really want to brighten up a room, try it as the primary colour!

Kitchen

Kitchen

Kitchens/Dining Room

Kitchens, just by their very nature, are the hub of every household, constantly being utilised to keep our families adequately nourished and healthily ticking over. Modern-day kitchens are also more and more the part of the house where our families have an opportunity to spend time together…be it children studying at the dining table whilst we prepare dinner, sitting down for dinner with family or friends, having a mid-morning cup of coffee or even just doing the dishes together. Whatever its function this hive of activity is an important part of our busy lifestyles and the best-planned kitchens will exude a welcoming feel for everyone.

So, could your kitchen do with some home-improvements? Whether it's something as simple as a fresh coat of paint, or something more radical like replacing units or extending space – your kitchen is a treasured area of your house and deserves some attention.

Create a Comfy Zone

If your space allows, it's lovely to have an area of the kitchen where people can sit in comfort – be it beanbags, two-seater sofas or some other comfy-seat option. It'll attract more of your family into the kitchen, encouraging more time together.

Create an Island!

To make your kitchen as sociable and practical environment as possible, if you have room then why not install an island unit. This will create an extra practical component as a preparation area, breakfast bar, dishing-up area, etc – as well as somewhere to sit and chat, have a relaxing cup of coffee, or sit and read a book. It might even bring teenagers in to kitchen, instead of being holed-up in their rooms, (you never know)! Placement of your island unit should be as central as possible to be in an optimum position for eating and cooking.

Disguise Your Appliances

If you don't like the stark glare of your fridge freezer, dishwasher or other 'white goods', then you could look into finding appropriately sized cabinet doors to match your kitchen. Covering your appliances will have the effect of blending and streamlining your kitchen.

Flooring

Above any other consideration, your kitchen floor needs to be robust! Needing to stand up to lots of foot-traffic, food spills, dropped cutlery and cooking utensils, pets, children, etc – your flooring will go through some punishing times, so choose with your individual household traffic volumes in mind.

Ceramic & Porcelain Tiles

Give your kitchen floor a real treat and go for the beauty and resilience of ceramic or porcelain tiles. There are literally hundreds of different styles and colours, so you'll be sure to find something that's perfect for your kitchen needs... whether you go for the elegance of marble-effect and high-gloss, the beauty of intricate mosaic tiles, the warmth and comfort of terracotta or the stylish inspiration of Italian fresco tiles.

When choosing your tiles take into consideration the size of your kitchen. Smaller tiles for smaller kitchens doesn't necessarily follow – if you've too many tiles and grout lines, this can make your space look smaller and make your flooring look too 'busy'. Take some advice if you're not sure – you'll most probably be intending for the floor to be there long-term, so making the right choice is vital.

Wooden Floors

If wood appeals to you for a natural look, then think about laying a hardwood floor. Unless you have enough knowledge about the different types of wood, then it's an idea to get some professional advice. To make the floor practical as well as beautiful, it should be finished with a good quality-waterproofing product.

Vinyl Floors

If your budget is a little on the stretched side then expensive flooring doesn't need to be at the top of your list. If you're concentrating on improving your kitchen at eye-level, flooring can be looked at from a more affordable perspective. Vinyl flooring comes in a sheet or square format, with an extensive range of textures, styles and colours. A versatile and easy to clean option, the wide range of varieties will make it easy for you to match to your kitchen.

Fresh Fruit & Flowers

A really affordable and easy way to give your kitchen an instant boost! A colourful and fragrant collection of fruits and/or a beautiful vase of flowers will make your kitchen look pleasantly inviting. Go for glass or open-weave fruit bowls, so that you can make the most out of displaying your fruit.

Freshen Up The Walls

Give your kitchen an instant lift by painting it! You can opt for a more daring colour, or just give it a new coat of the same colour. Either way you'll revitalise the look and energy of your kitchen. If you're changing the colour, think about what you want to achieve, e.g. do you want to lighten up your kitchen or go for a warm and homely look. Maybe try a feature wall of a deeper, bolder colour, contrasted by lighter, calm colours.

Go Granite!

Add a touch of elegance and luxury to your kitchen and choose granite for your kitchen worktops. Good quality granite is stunning to look at, as well as being durable. It costs more than traditional worktops and it requires a bit more care and maintenance, but its quality and longevity make it a worthwhile investment. Granite comes in a wide range of patterns and colours. Source a reputable supplier and fitter for the best results.

Kitchen Cabinets

To replace or not to replace… that may well be the question! Replacing them is likely going to be the more expensive of the two options, so it's worth considering whether they are worth 'pepping-up', giving them a fresh, new look.

To help your decision making process have a good think about what sort of look you want for your kitchen, e.g. do you want clean, modern lines – or are you more of a cosy, country kitchen kind of person? Picture yourself preparing your dinner, having coffee with your friends or just sitting peacefully and taking some timeout – what do you want surrounding you? Remember that you're improving for YOU not for a prospective buyer, so ignore any nagging voices that tell you to go with what's 'in-vogue'.

If you're happy with the actual style of your cabinets, but fancy a different colour, with maybe a change of handle accessory or a different paint effect – then refinishing your existing cabinets could be the route for you to go. This option will also give you greater versatility and a real sense of your kitchen being absolutely unique. Just remember that refinishing will take more time and effort, so take into consideration what work levels would be involved and how practicable that is for you.

If, on the other hand, you look around your kitchen and feel that no amount of accesorising and freshening-up will get you the look that you're after, then it's probably worth replacing them – budget allowing.

Kitchen-Diner Alterations

New-builds are largely built with kitchen-diners, maximising the space and following the modern idea of the kitchen being the nerve-centre of the home.

If you live in a house where the kitchen and dining room are next to each other, but with a separating wall – then you might want to consider opening up the space by knocking the wall through and making the two rooms into a kitchen-diner. Naturally, this will mean that your kitchen units will need to be moved, replaced or added to – so if that's not an option, you could still make a difference by removing the upper part of the adjoining wall to create a more sociable environment.

Kitchen Re-fits

If your heart is set on redesigning your kitchen and you can afford to do it, then this is a great opportunity for you to have your own tailor-made dream! If you've got the space, you may opt for a freestanding kitchen with a mixture of styles and effects – or you may go for the allure of a streamlined fitted kitchen, made especially to make the best use of any awkward corners or dead space.

If you're hyper-focused and know exactly what you want for your kitchen, you'll most probably be able to create your perfect room without any major dramas. Check your ideas out with your nearest and dearest and it's a good idea to get a professional opinion before you commit to buying. If you're the type of person who has a hard time choosing which brand of toilet paper to buy at the supermarket, then you're going to need the time and space to really think about what you want. And walking into Ikea with hundreds of different styles and ideas is most likely not a good idea for you... not unless you're prepared to go into 'overwhelm'!

One way to tackle this issue is to utilise the services of kitchen suppliers and their design software, which is available in most outfitters. All you need to do is take the dimensions of your kitchen, pick some kitchen styles that you like and the staff will assist you in building your kitchen – giving you a 3D perspective of how it will look in reality. However, before you commit to a purchase, ensure that your supplier has taken exact measurements – just to rule out any measuring errors.

Lighting

Lighting can really make or break the ambience of your kitchen, especially if it's also a diner. Part of your improvements could include re-hauling your kitchen lighting to give you a number of looks, styles and function options.

As well as having spot or strip lighting, include lights underneath your wall cabinets. This will give direct light to smaller areas, allowing functional activities without the glare of overhead lighting.

When you're cooking a big dinner and the kitchen is a hive of activity, good quality overhead lighting is a must.

To get the best of both worlds, have your overhead lights on different circuits so that you can control the level of light easily; allowing you to transform stark, bright functional lighting into softer, more intimate lighting for sitting down to dinner.

Treat your kitchen dining area to a tasteful decorative pendant light fitting, one with a dimmer switch is preferable so that you can create an intimate dining area – or if the table is being used for something more functional such as studying, it can be turned up.

Mucky Marks!

Practically a cost-free improvement for your kitchen – tackle old stains and marks from your kitchen. It might not feel like a dynamic move, but it's a vital one in bringing your kitchen up to scratch!

Stainless Steel

Remove unsightly marks from stainless steal by using a little WD-40 on a soft cloth. Rub the marks gently and then wipe over the top with a dry piece of the soft cloth.

Kitchen Counters

Remove stubborn marks from marble, Formica or plastic kitchen counters; gently scour with a paste of bicarbonate of soda and water.

Kitchen Tiles

Clean grubby, stained kitchen tiles with a paste made from bicarbonate of soda and a little bleach. Apply and scrub, then rinse off thoroughly.

White Porcelain Sinks

Revitalise a stained and yellowed white porcelain sink by making a solution of 65ml of bicarbonate of soda, 125 ml bleach and 1 litre of warm water. Mix the ingredients together well and apply to the sink with a sponge. Leave for 10 minutes and then rinse thoroughly. Buff your sink with a dry cloth.

Music Maestro!

Inject some music into your kitchen with a good sound system and speakers, (concealed or wall-mounted). That way you can enjoy your favourite music whilst you prepare dinner, small children can dance to their favourite nursery rhymes, dinner parties can be accompanied by low-level soft music choices or you can simply have a dance around your kitchen when the mood takes you!

On The Tiles!

A common issue in kitchens that have been around for a while, old-fashioned or tired looking tiles! Tiles patterned with stencils of kettles, jugs, vases of flowers or teapots may be your thing – but they might also be something that makes you cringe every time you look at them. Or maybe your tiles just need freshening up with a new colour. Whichever scenario applies, if replacing them isn't an option at the moment – then simply buy some tile paint, don your painting gear and breathe some new life into them!

Alternatively, if changing your tiles is an option then shop around and find something that inspires you. You'll find an extensive amount of choice when it comes to style, texture and colour; and there'll be plenty of help out there if you need a little advice and direction.

Whether you're painting or replacing you tiles, if your kitchen lacks a bit of light then go for a lighter/brighter colour – you'll be surprised at how much you'll open up the space by simply opening up your colour palette.

Out with the Old

We clear out our wardrobes of garments that we no longer wear, or that are out of fashion – so why not apply this rule to our kitchens? You know… the blender that's gathering dust on top of your fridge or the coffee grinder that's been stuffed at the back of a cupboard for the last 3 years?

Your kitchen may be more cluttered than you realise, so it's time for a clear out! Pick out what you don't want and determine whether to sell, bin or donate each item. It's a simple step to take, but it will help your overall improvements by clearing space and removing clutter.

Seating

Look at the seating in your kitchen – how does it measure up to the look you want to achieve? Even if you can't afford to buy a new dining table and chairs, maybe you could re-cover your existing chairs or stain/paint them if they're wooden. Have a look at alternative seating options for your kitchen/dining area, such as wooden benches, breakfast-bar stools, bucket seats, etc.

Space Savers

Great storage is vital, especially if space is an issue for you. Here are a few smart storage ideas to make your improvements a lot more effective: -

*   If you're struggling for space to store pots and pans, consider whether they can be suspended from a wall or ceiling.

*   Utilise wall space and erect shelving for cookbooks, storage tins and other items.

*   Carousels fitted into corner cupboards can make the most of the most hard-to-reach spaces – whilst also ensuring that you can see exactly what's in there… no more tins of soup dating back a decade!

*   Consider layered storage rack options for inside cupboards – these can be for food, crockery or baking and cooking materials.

* Store containers by size, stacking the smaller sizes inside the bigger sizes.

* Square or oblong containers are easier to store and take up less space than their round counterparts.

* Save drawer space by hanging larger cooking utensils on hooks, either on the wall or on the inside of a cupboard.

* Position handy items such as paper-towel dispensers, tea-towel hooks and plastic bag and cling-wrap dispensers on walls or on the outside of cupboards. These can save space as well as avoiding having to wrestle with packaging with wet or sticky hands!

Taps

For a really simple way to jazz up your kitchen sink, invest in some good quality taps. Go for a different style, colour or veneer – something that will give you the feeling of a brand new sink! If you have mixer-taps then a change to better quality taps may well improve temperature control and water pressure.

Top-to-Bottom Blinds

If you want a bit of privacy and a way to control the amount of light that comes through your kitchen window, top-to-bottom blinds are the most versatile option. They're easy to install and they don't look too fussy either. Pick a colour that will compliment your overall colour scheme.

Warm It Up

If you want your kitchen to be the central hub of the house, then it needs to be warm and inviting – not only in it's look but in terms of its temperature! So, if your kitchen is little on the chilly or draughty side then you might want to consider underfloor heating, or radiators. Sitting shivering with thick jumpers on is hardly conducive to a bustlingly sociable kitchen!

Lounge

Lounge

Lounge

Our lounges are the part of the house where everyone retires to at one time of the day or another. It's the part of our homes where we like to congregate, relax and spend quality time together; as well as where we receive company.

Our lounges are the place where we can kick back with a cup of tea or coffee, stretch our feet out and forget about the world outside…where we sit down as a family and watch our favourite programmes…where we curl up on the sofa with our favourite book…and where we sit with friends and family, having a drink, playing a game or putting the world-to-rights.

Our living rooms have a world of different functions, making it one of the most important rooms in the house; that being the case, it's probably one of the areas of the house that needs updating and improving above all the rest.

Accessories

Add your own unique touch with accessories and create an environment that reflects yours and your family's personalities - making it a perfect place for you to retreat to and relax and to welcome in your friends.

Make sure that accessories compliment or contrast well with your chosen style, theme and colour scheme.

Give your lounge a three-dimensional feel and add stylishly contrasting textures… for instance, soft furnishings can be a mixture of leather, faux-fur, velvet, silk, etc.

Replacing simple hardware accessories within your lounge can give it a fabulous mini-facelift – such as light switches, sockets, door handles, trims, etc.

Add throws and cushions to sofas and arm chairs, especially if they're a little worn and you can't afford new furnishings just yet.

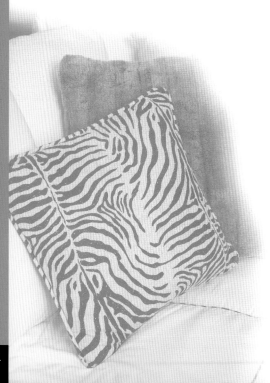

Choose one stylish and beautiful piece of art to give your lounge a fabulous focal point.

If you have children, make sure that you have at least one picture of them in your lounge. It's a subtle way of showing them how integral they are to the household and subconsciously they'll take that in. If you want to move away from typical family photos then think about using black and white prints, or having a picture transferred onto a large canvas.

If you don't want to go with mainstream looks, opting instead for something a little different – try art and design shows, craft fairs, markets, auctions, antique shops… even car boot sales.

If you don't want to go with mainstream looks, opting instead for something a little different – try art and design shows, craft fairs, markets, auctions, antique shops… even car boot sales.

If you enjoy more zen-like surroundings, the trickling sound of an indoor water feature is a great way of injecting a feeling of calm and tranquility. It's also considered a way of encouraging good energy from a feng-shui perspective.

Make use of the space you have without going over-the-top. Accessorising with candles, vases, artwork, photos, ornaments, etc can look great – but if you overload your surfaces it'll just look too busy and your favourite pieces will get lost in all the other items surrounding them.

If you suspect that you're a little on the excessive side, then take away your least favourite accessories and leave a few carefully chosen items – you might well be pleasantly surprised. And there'll be less dusting too!

Lounge

Rugs

Rugs are wonderfully versatile; they can be used to add colour, texture, comfort and warmth to a room, as well as being able create the illusion of different areas within a space – perhaps defining the territory between the lounge and the dining area.

There are a number of ways in which the addition of a rug can improve a room, for instance, if you have a large lounge with a wooden floor, a large rug can be placed in the centre, giving colour to the room, creating a visual contrast around the borders and drawing the eye to the space within which the rug lies. Or you may want to add a faux-fur rug directly in front of a fireplace to give your living room a classically warm feeling.

Whether you choose a patterned or colourful rug, or one that remains neutral, is a matter of personal choice and style.

Be Sales-Savvy

If you're planning to make big changes to your lounge, changes that include significant items of furniture, then it's a good idea to wait for the sales. You could get your preferred style of sofa for half the price if you wait for the right time. Use price comparison sites over the internet, to ensure that you're really getting the best deal too.

Carpeted Floors

If the carpet in your lounge is looking a bit on the tired side, then you've a few options – steam clean it yourself, have it professionally cleaned or take it up and replace it with a new carpet. Or if you're lucky and you fancy a complete change, you might have floorboards underneath that can be sanded and polished – adding a rug for a splash of warmth and colour.

Clutter

Identify areas of the lounge that tend to attract clutter and address them. Either introduce racks or storage options or fill the space with something decorative that will discourage those that leave the clutter. If other members of the household continue to leave clutter in the area, then stick to your no-clutter-rule and confront the issue directly.

Dressing Windows

The way in which you dress your windows will have a dramatic effect on the overall look of your lounge, so changing your style of window dressing is a surefire way to make a stunning improvement to your bedroom.

Your preferred style of window dressing will naturally be a matter of personal taste, but it's also important to select a look that suits the style, positioning and function of your windows – as well as matching the overall mood and theme of your lounge. For instance, if you're looking for a minimalist, streamlined feel then simple Venetian blinds may be what you're looking for – but it may not suit the size of the window, making it look too bland and boring.

So to help you avoid making some potentially expensive mistakes, here are a few pointers to help you in your decision making process:-

* Does the window actually need dressing? Maybe you have a beautifully decorative architecture to a window that doesn't need anything extra adding to it. In which case, maybe undressing your window is the key to improving your lounge!

* Does the dressing for your window need to decorative, functional or a mixture of both?

* What level of privacy do you need your window dressings to give you?

* What level of light does your lounge need and how will your window dressing affect this? This may also be dependant on the direction of the sun in relation to your lounge.

Consider the positioning of the sun in choosing the fabrics for your windows. Some fabrics will fade over time if exposed to strong sunlight. What feel do you want to create in your lounge and how do your window dressings fit in with this?

Lounge

Consider existing furnishings, colour schemes, flooring and accessories. Think carefully about the size and style of the window itself and what fabrics and trimmings would be best suited. For example, smaller windows may be better served by using roller or Roman blinds.

Fresh Fruit & Flowers
A really affordable and easy way to give your lounge an instant boost! A colourful and fragrant collection of fruits and/or a beautiful vase of flowers will make the room look pleasantly inviting. Go for glass or open-weave fruit bowls, so that you can make the most out of displaying your fruit.

Freshen Up The Walls
Give your lounge an instant lift by painting it! You can opt for a more daring colour, or just give it a new coat of the same colour. Either way you'll revitalise the look and energy of your living room.

If you're changing the colour, think about what you want to achieve, e.g. do you want to lighten up your lounge or go for a more warm and homely look. Maybe try a feature wall of a deeper, bolder colour, contrasted by lighter, calmer colours.

Lounge

Have a Feature Wall

If you want to make a bold statement in your lounge, then a feature wall just might be for you - particularly if your usual colour scheme leans towards a more neutral look and you want to be a bit more daring in your colour choice. A feature wall allows you to experiment with more vibrant colours or wallpaper patterns without overwhelming the rest of the room. It's a quick and easy way of injecting a burst of personality into your lounge area and if you hate it, then it's only one wall that you have to paint or wallpaper over!

When choosing your feature wall it's a good idea to pick an uninterrupted wall space, i.e. with no doors and windows to break the colour or pattern – so this could be the wall that first meets the eye when walking into your lounge area. Equally chimneybreasts and alcoves can take brighter, bolder colours and patterns.

Heat-Up Your Fireplace!

The fireplace is the focal point of the lounge area, so if this is to be part of your improvement plans then it's vital to combine functionality with elegance and style.

Choosing a new fireplace for your lounge will be an incredibly important decision - and the colour scheme, style and feel of your living room will have the greatest impact on your choice. See it as being akin to picking a sofa, carpet or new wallpaper – you wouldn't just stick any old-thing in your lounge, you'd want it to match the mood and ambience of the room.

If your actual fire isn't the problem, but the surround is, then you can shop for this separately. There are some magnificent choices available, so shop around different suppliers and come up with a shortlist of your favourite styles before you make your final choice.

Follow the health and safety directions in relation to the installation of your new fireplace and ensure that a registered professional deals with connecting and disconnecting energy supplies.

Lounge

49

Lighting

Changing the way that you choose to light your lounge can change the mood dramatically. Bright overhead lights can give a stark, impersonal feel to your lounge area – but you might not want to get rid of them completely. Perhaps install a central light with a dimmer switch, so that the tone of lighting can be changed according to need.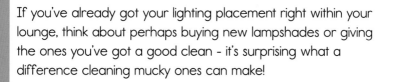

Freestanding lamps create pockets of light within a room without the light being too bright. This can be helpful for reading, watching television or just having a more ambient feel to your lounge.

If you've already got your lighting placement right within your lounge, think about perhaps buying new lampshades or giving the ones you've got a good clean - it's surprising what a difference cleaning mucky ones can make!

Lounging Around

If your lounge has an imbalance of bottoms-to-seats ratio, then there's an obvious improvement-need there! Of course, it could be as easy as buying in a few new armchairs, or an extra sofa to match your existing furniture – however, if space and/or finances are an issue then you'll need a solution that doesn't impinge too much on either of those issues.

If there is an imbalance going on it's quite likely that you have children in the house – well, on the basis that most children LOVE floor cushions/ beanbags, then why not invest in some for your lounge? They can be bought fairly cheaply and if you don't want them clogging-up your living room all day, then the cushions or beanbags can double up as seating in your children's rooms.

Nest of Tables

If you don't have the room for more than one coffee table in your lounge, then a nest of tables will help save space and also provide extra table surfaces when you need it.

Paper/Magazine Rack

If you don't already have one, a paper/magazine rack is a really simple lounge improvement idea. It'll tidy-up all your newspapers, magazines, comics and other publications that would normally live on the floor, underneath the sofa, or stuffed down the side of a chair! You can also buy multi-functioning racks that house remote controls and that act as mini-table tops too.

Patterns & Colour

If you're not overly keen on patterns or bright colours dominating your lounge, but you'd like to introduce a bit more 'life' into your living room, then why not try adding some colour and/or patterns by way of a rug, a throw or some carefully selected cushions? That way you can inject flashes of colour and vibrancy without overwhelming your room. It'll also ease you into becoming a bit more daring if you're not overly confident with more daring colour schemes and patterns.

Period Features & Furniture

If you have a home that still has some of it's period features, then why not bring out their original beauty and reclaim them? Fireplaces, doors, windows, floorboards, coving, skirting and other architectural features – all of which could bring an authentic feel and character to your lounge. Do your homework before you begin any work and establish what you can and can't do yourself, i.e. you may need to bring in a professional restorer for some items.

Apply this thinking for pieces of old or antique furniture too – tables, cabinets, lamps, sideboards, bureaus, etc. There will be lots that you can do for yourself, with a little hard graft and tender loving care. It'll be worth it if you want to recapture that original feel and elegance.

Lounge

Repair, Revamp or Replace?

Look objectively at your lounge and the items within it – what can be repaired or revamped; and what items are to be got rid of? If you've an irreplaceable, treasured heirloom then you may opt for having it restored; or moved to another room – likewise you may have some cheap and cheerful items that have had their day and that can be recycled or dumped. Make a list of what you want to keep and what's disposable. All the 'keep' items are going to become part of your improvements, so will need to be included in your considerations for your new style ideas and colour scheme.

Streamline Your Lounge

Maybe the contents of your lounge have grown with you barely noticing over the years – but when you look at it with your fresh, home-improvement eyes you'll discover a mixture of questionable holiday mementoes, dusty dried flowers, piles of books, burnt-down candle wicks, fussy ornaments, etc. If so, then it's time to have a clear out and streamline your room.

Toys

If space issues determine that there are children's toys in your lounge area, then organise them in storage baskets/bins or arrange them in a shelving unit to save space and maximise neatness.

Upholstering

You don't necessarily have to write-off your current soft furnishings, especially if you love their style. Consider the option of having your favourite pieces upholstered with new fabric instead of being lured into the 'seduction' of a new sofa!

Use Your Alcoves

If lack of space and too much clutter are issues within your lounge, then make use of any wall alcoves by erecting shelving or fitted cupboards. You can also use shelving in alcoves to showcase loved ornaments, pictures or other possessions. If you have window alcoves that are currently housing dead-space, think about making them into seating areas with padded seating and plush cushions.

Bedrooms

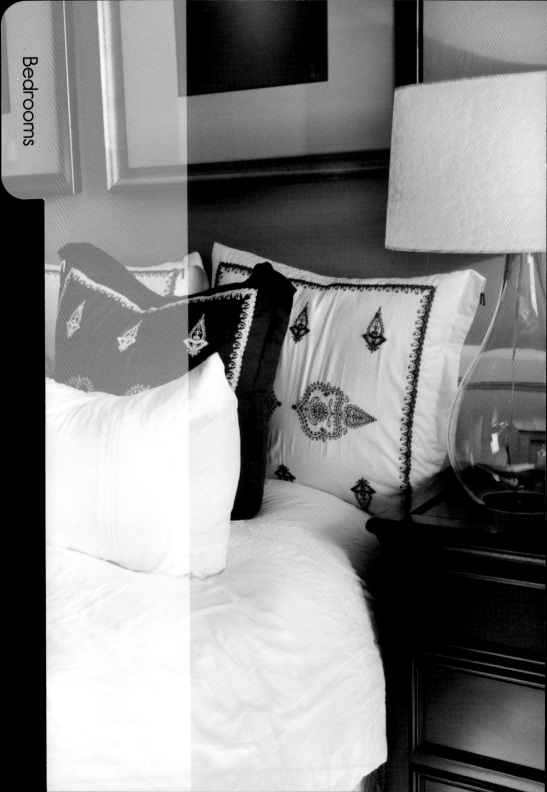

Bedroom

Our bedrooms are the ultimate peaceful haven in our homes and the heart of our relationships; an essential space for rest, rejuvenation and sleep; as well as a personal, peaceful place to unwind and let go of the stresses of the day. When we are ill, our bedrooms are also where we take time out to heal and return to good health.

Adult bedrooms are an integral place for relaxation, intimacy and love; or if you're single, a special place to snuggle up in private and read a good book before settling down to a restful night's sleep. Children's bedrooms are a space for playing, a place to house treasured toys, show off their favourite duvet covers and accessories to friends and to cuddle up for a bedtime story. And of course, teenage bedrooms are the ultimate escape from parents and the world!

Bedrooms are the one place in the house where we feel that we can place our own personal stamp in terms of style and colour scheme – and so they should be! If the rest of the house matches a flowing colour scheme, due to the communal aspect of the rooms, then bedrooms are a perfect place for self-expression. So if the bedrooms in your house could do with a bit of an overhaul, then look no further!

Adult Bedrooms

Beginnings...Style & Atmosphere

When you're considering what improvements you want to make to your bedroom, begin by starting with the style and mood that you want your bedroom to have, e.g. minimalist, oriental, rustic, classic, etc. Your choice of style will help you in deciding the colours, fabrics and furniture that you choose for your bedroom.

Carpets & Rugs – Treat Your Feet!

One of the most wonderful feelings in the morning is to get out of bed and place your feet directly onto a luxuriously thick carpet or rug. Lending themselves to a real warm and homely feel, comfy carpets and rugs allow us to literally tread softly around our bedroom!

So as a really indulgent part of your home improvement, investing in a plush new carpet or something like a faux-fur rug could be just what your bedrooms needs.

Choosing a Colour Scheme

Don't get too stuck on the colour scheme for your bedroom being centred on the existing colour of your walls. Walls can be painted after all! If you want a radical change to take place, be a little more adventurous and pick out a favourite curtain fabric, duvet cover, rug or even lampshade as your colour and style inspiration.

It might feel a little scary basing it on so little to start with, but once you get into the swing of things you'll have a great time matching everything together.

If this isn't your forte, then ask for some help from either a friend or family member. We're not all blessed with interior design know-how, so flex your creative-muscles with the help of someone you trust.

Create a Quiet Corner

If you have the room, set aside a corner or alcove in your bedroom where you can retreat to and have some well-earned peace and quiet. It can be somewhere that you choose to read, meditate or simply have some quiet time doing nothing. Kit the area out with something comfortable for you to seat yourself and surround yourself with items that make you feel safe, secure and relaxed.

De-clutter

First and foremost, is your bedroom an environment for calm and wellbeing? Or is it more akin to rest and disorder? If it's the latter of the two then chances are that you have too much clutter in your bedroom. So, for a really simple and cost-free improvement option, get rid of your clutter!

Take a good look at all the surfaces in the room, i.e. anything that will act as a dumping ground for things that haven't made it to their rightful resting place. Look at bedside tables, chests of drawers, dressing tables, chairs, bedsteads, etc. Starting with one surface at a time, take off all the items and either put them away, give them charity or get rid of them.

If your bedroom is a home for lots of knick-knacks, then you need to decide whether they are adding value to your room or making it more of a cluttered, dusting nightmare! Again, there's no right or wrong answer to this one – because if your knick-knacks add to making your bedroom feel like your own personal sanctuary, then no-one has the right to tell you that they shouldn't be there.

If, on the other hand, your knick-knacks have crept up on you a little and you actually feel that they detract from the overall feel that you want for your bedroom, then you can either move them out to another room, box them up in a 'memorabilia-style' box or throw them out.

Or maybe you can come up with a compromise somewhere between the two; keeping items that have significant personal meaning to you and storing the rest away.

Dim The Lights!

Create a relaxing and ambient feeling to your bedroom by installing a light with a dimmer switch. This will give you the choice of a brighter light for reading, or gentler lighting for relaxing or creating a bit of romance with your partner. Alternatively, adorn your bedroom with attractive lamps, with low wattage or coloured bulbs. For instance, a terracotta or peach coloured lamp will give your room a much softer glow, creating a warmer feel.

For reading in bed, save room by the side of your bed by purchasing clip-on lights that you can affix to your bedposts.

Dressing Windows

The way in which you dress your windows will have a dramatic effect on the overall look of your bedroom, so changing your style of window dressing is a surefire way to make a stunning improvement to your bedroom.

Your preferred style of window dressing will naturally be a matter of personal taste, but it's also important to select a look that suits the style, positioning and function of your windows – as well as matching the overall mood and theme of your bedroom. For instance, if you're looking for a sumptuous, romantic feel then volumes of beautiful, draping fabric may be the look that you're looking for – but it may not suit the size of the window, overwhelming it and blocking out too much light.

So to help you avoid making some potentially expensive mistakes, here are a few pointers to help you in your decision making process:-

Does the window actually need dressing? Maybe you have a beautifully decorative architecture to a window that doesn't need anything extra adding to it. In which case, maybe undressing your window is the key to improving your bedroom!

*   Does the dressing for your window need to decorative, functional or a mixture of both?

*   What level of privacy do you need your window dressings to give you?

*   What level of light does your bedroom need and how will your window dressing affect this? This may also be dependant on the direction of the sun in relation to your bedroom.

Consider the positioning of the sun in choosing the fabrics for your windows. Some fabrics will fade over time if exposed to strong sunlight.

What feel do you want to create in your bedroom and how do your window dressings fit in with this? Consider existing furnishings, colour schemes, flooring and accessories.

Think carefully about the size and style of the window itself and what fabrics and trimmings would be best suited. For example, smaller windows may be better served by roller or roman blinds.

Fabrics

Have some fun with fabrics … Depending on the style and theme you want your bedroom to convey, fabrics can add a sense of elegance, fun, luxury and of course, good old-fashioned romance. Think about sumptuous, rich velvets, sensuous silks, delicate lace, warm damasks, luxurious suede, versatile toile and faux fur & leather. All of which come in an endless variety of colours, prints, patterns and textures. Be as creative as you want to be - using your fabrics for your bedding, throws, chairs, chaise-longues, cushions, sofas, rugs, curtains, etc.

Fabulous Bed!

Your bed takes centre stage your bedroom, so it should stand out as your main feature. Make your bed look fabulous; something that anyone would want to sink into!

A really simple way to improve your bedroom is to buy really good quality bed linen for maximum comfort and a great look. Invest in a duvet that is one size bigger than the bed, as this will give it a really plush and luxurious feel – as well as looking temptingly inviting!

Feature Wall

Create a feature in your room by choosing one wall - perhaps the headboard wall, or the main wall of the room – to paint in a rich accent colour or decorate with elaborate wallpaper. This will draw attention to this part of the room and create a stunning contrast to the rest of the walls.

Flattering Floor Space

If your bedroom colour scheme is neutral or a little on the cold side, then why not add a little warmth and vibrancy by adding a bright or warm coloured rug by the side of your bed? Or, if your room can take it, how about a patterned rug? It's an easy way of adding a subtle touch of colour without being overwhelming.

Headboards & Bedsteads

Liven-up the focal point of your bedroom and give your bed a fabulous new headboard or bedstead. Whether you choose a bright, snazzy padded cover to top your bed or a beautifully designed iron bedstead to give it a classic feel… either way you'll be sure to be bringing a wonderful new element to your bedroom.

Televisions

This is a real bone of contention for most interior designer 'types'. "No, no, no!" – being the general consensus! In terms of relaxation and rest, watching high-octane action or dramas before you go to sleep certainly isn't conducive to a good night's sleep. Research tells us that it's likely to make us restless and unable to drift as easily into a deeper, more restful sleep. Television also tends to stop us from reading and/or spending more quality time with our partners. So, it's worth considering whether removing your television from your bedroom is a worthwhile improvement in terms of the potential for your relationships, health and general wellbeing.

That said, this book is all about personal choice and maybe watching television in your bedroom is a real treat for you; so stay with what's true to your vision of bedroom-bliss and not what is prescribed for you. If you can, place your television in a cupboard or somewhere that you can have it hidden when it's not in use – just in the interests of streamlining your room.

Storage/Space Saving Tips

Great storage is a must for bedrooms, especially if space is an issue for you. As aesthetics are important for your bedroom, good storage should be versatile and where possible, concealed – so do your homework into adaptable storage options. Here are a few pointers to make your improvements more effective: -

* Use your wall space and erect some shelving to display decorative items, photos or books.

* For shelves that are both deep and narrow, use appropriately sized storage baskets to store smaller items. This will allow you to slide the baskets out and search for items without knocking other things over.

* Where possible, use the tops of wardrobes or underneath beds to keep out of season clothes, linen or seasonal duvets. There are plenty of sealable storage products to keep you items dust-free and clean.

* Concealed storage will be of great appeal for bedroom organisation, so finding items that are dual-purpose, such as a table with draws underneath, are key to your bedroom aesthetics.

* Shelving above eye-level, in a wardrobe or cupboard, should be no more than 12 inches deep. Anything deeper will mean that you're unable to see what you've stored.

* Items stored between waist and eye-level should be things that are either in season or used on a regular basis. Items that are either out of season or used infrequently can be stored at a higher/lower level or out of direct vision.

* If you've room on a wall or cabinet near to your mirror, screw in hooks to hang your hairdryer, curlers or straighteners. This saves space and valuable time, not having a to tackle untangling wires and plugs every morning.

* If you have lots of jewellery but find that you only use certain pieces, it could be because you can't see the whole range of what you have. Jewellery 'trees' are really useful for hanging necklaces and bracelets, making them more visible and as a storage option they look pretty into the bargain!

Children's Bedrooms

Beginnings...Get Their Input

Involve your children in the process of improving their bedroom and give them some power in making decisions – this will keep them interested and will be more of an incentive for keeping their bedroom tidy!

Work to make your children's rooms attractive and exciting to them. Favourite characters, colours, themes, stickers and materials are all key to giving them a bedroom that they will be chuffed-to-bits with. Don't be afraid of bright colours – you might love the more neutral, subtle look; but children are usually more motivated by daring 'out-there' colours. Even appropriate storage options can be found in bright, modern and child-pleasing designs and colours.

Think carefully about wallpaper featuring their favourite characters of the 'moment', children can grow out of them pretty quickly, making it feel like a bit of a wasted exercise. If your children are insistent that they want their chosen characters as part of their bedroom improvements, then how about compromising with framed pictures, bedspreads and other accessories featuring their choices instead? That way they can have a backdrop that won't be subject to fickle changes!

Most important of all, remember that it's THEIR room, not yours!

Blackout Blinds

An ingenious invention – blackout blinds are the answer to those light nights in the summer, when your children are convinced that it's still daytime and that it's too early to go to sleep! They also work well for early morning light. Research has shown that sleep achieved in darkness is better quality than sleep achieved with light present – so your children will feel more refreshed into the bargain.

Having the benefit of promoting sleep, blackout blinds are also perfect for babies' rooms. Not necessarily so great for teenagers rooms though … not if you want to see them before lunchtime!

Bookcases

It's all about the television, the PlayStation, the PSP, the DVD or CD player… right? Well, why not get back to some good old-fashioned basics in your children's rooms by adding a bookcase. Encourage them to re-discover a love for books and involve them in placing books on the shelves and showing them how to take care of them. It's a childhood pleasure that will make a real improvement to their lives, not just to their bedrooms.

Bookcases can also be used to showcase your children's favourite treasures too, so it's another way in which they can get pleasure out of the more simple things in life.

Children's Artwork

If your children love painting, drawing and colouring then why not let them celebrate their achievements, by hanging some string along a wall and using pegs to hang their artwork up? This will give them a real sense of pride, whilst keeping their artwork in tact and not stuffed, forgotten in drawers.

Door Hooks

Simple but effective – improve the look of your children's rooms by giving them somewhere to hang up their dressing gowns, nightwear, bags and any other item that might usually live on the floor or on the back of a chair! Add some hooks to the back of their door or on the side of a wall – buy them in a bright, decorative colour, or decorate them with something like a piece of tinsel to make them a bit more fun.

Exciting Lighting!

For children's rooms spotlights are great for bright lighting, as well as stand-alone spot-lamps for when they're reading their books at night. Coloured bulbs are also a popular choice for children – they'll love being able to create a completely different feel to their bedroom. There are also plenty of retail outlets that stock fabulous multi-coloured flashing disco-style lights, neon lamps, lava lamps, fairy lights coming in the form of butterflies, love-hearts, dragonflies, footballs… the choices are endless. Perfect for a child's room if you've not got a huge budget but want to create a new look for your children's bedrooms.

Floor Space

The greater the floor space in children's rooms the better. Like adults, children need their rooms to be the one place in the house that they can call their own. Giving your children enough floor space means that they can play with treasured toys and have room to have their favourite friends over to play. For pre-school children, room for something like a miniature table and chairs will provide them somewhere to play with arts and crafts, or to have a tea party - hours of delight and fun! To give your children as much floor space as possible, storage will be an important consideration. Whether it be bright, plastic storage boxes for toys and games, or furniture – there are plenty of retailers that will supply a wide range of choices to make your children's bedrooms more user-friendly.

Make it Multi-Functional

Children absolutely love pieces of furniture that have more than one purpose to them. Bedsteads and headboards that can have fluffy fairy lights threaded through them, sofa beds providing seating for friends as well as sleep-over options, a divan holding important and top-secret toys in it's drawers, cubbyholes for favourite books or a built-in alcove underneath a bunk bed housing a chair, table, bookcase and computer for older children. Whatever your choices, think about how your children's furniture will serve them for the immediate term and as they get older. If your children are pre-school age then it's likely that you'll need to re-jig their rooms as they get older, but if they're aged eight or older then it's worth thinking carefully about how any changes will convert as they move into secondary school.

Make it a Sleepy Haven

Children's lives these days are busy, busy, busy! School, football, netball, hockey, rugby, karate, dance classes, music practice, play-dates, parties, school trips… it's a never ending schedule of 'doing'. So, it's vital that their bedrooms are a place where they can truly relax and be peaceful, allowing them to wind down and not be further stimulated. At night, bedside lamps give off a nice dimmed light in the room, so that children can read before they go to sleep, but also signaling that it's bedtime and time for them to get some much-needed shut-eye. Alternatively, have their main light on a dimmer switch, so that you can dim their lighting at bedtime.

For younger children, televisions, computers and games consoles are not a good idea – so be firm and have them in more communal areas. For older children/teenagers, this rule might not be so easy to apply, so ensure that the rest of their rooms are conducive to a tranquil ambience.

One-Wall-Rule

If you're locked in a battle about posters being plastered all over bedroom walls, (oh, the pain of removing sticky-tape and Blu-tack!), then it's worth considering a one-wall-rule, i.e. they can put up what they like on ONE wall.

Paint a Mural

If you're struggling for inspiration for your children's rooms and you have an artistic streak, how about painting them a mural on their main wall? A princesses' castle within a land of winding roads and magical characters, a luscious green rainforest filled with tropical animals or a stunning ocean scene with beautiful and mysterious sea creatures… the possibilities are endless. Your children will love watching the transformation evolve and they'll revel in having a bedroom that's unique to them. If a full-sized mural feels a bit overwhelming then you can always try your hand at stenciling instead, complimented by colourful accessories.

Teenagers

Teenagers like to feel that they have a sense of being individual and of gaining a bit more power over their lives. One of the ways in which you can allow teenagers to achieve this is to allow them some creative flexibility in their bedrooms. It might horrify you that your teenager wants to paint their walls black and red, but as long as you can paint over what their preferences are, (once they're ready for you to do so), and they're not knocking chunks out of the walls, then why not let them experiment and develop their own tastes? Its all part and parcel of them growing up.
If this is a little too risqué for your liking and you're a little worried about your teenagers taking their decorative freedom too far, ask them to sit and plan out their ideas and discuss them in realistic terms. Take them shopping for their accessories and get them to help paint the room, so that they can appreciate the work that goes into decorating. Remember, that it's vital to set aside your own personal likes and dislikes on this one - they've got to sleep in there, not you…and it's a small price to pay for a contented teenager!

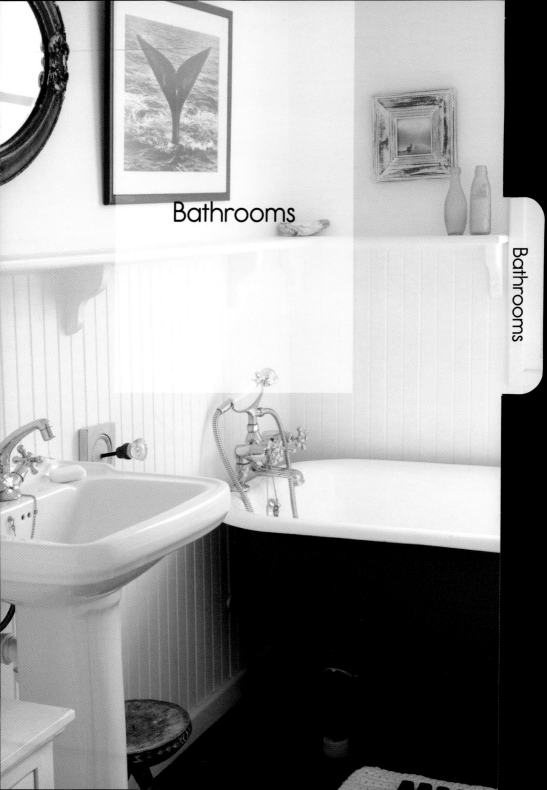

Bathrooms

Bathrooms

Our bathrooms provide space for all our grooming and personal hygiene needs, playing host to all sorts of weird and wonderful products, beauty routines, personal quirks and rituals! This room is undeniably one of the hardest-working rooms in your home, needing to be multi-functional in terms of different needs at different times. When improving our bathrooms we need to be able to strike a balance between eye-pleasing aesthetics and practicality in terms of plumbing, user-friendly designs, free-flowing space, ample storage and all our daily ablution needs! On a busy morning the bathroom needs to be a picture of organisational perfection with products being housed in the right place, enough towels being available and dry, a well functioning bath or hot shower, good ventilation, a non-leaky shower curtain or shower stall… basically, it needs to be all things to all members of our home. On the opposite end of the scale, our bathrooms should also be a warm and inviting sanctuary; somewhere that we want to spend time taking a luxuriously long bath surrounded by candles and soft music, somewhere that we can soothe ourselves and unwind in peace, quiet and privacy.

By re-vamping or adding in new cabinets, bathroom suites, accessories, floorings and décor, you can completely change the look and ambience of your bathroom. So, if part of your home-improvement plans involves spicing up your bathroom, here are some pointers to help you.

Beginnings – What Do You Want?

Before you begin planning your changes, have a think about what you don't like about your existing bathroom and write your thoughts down, e.g. it's too dark, there's not enough storage, the layout of the bathroom makes the space cramped, the tiles need re-grouting, etc. That way you can take stock of what you'd like to achieve and see how it fits in with your budget.

Involve your family and see what they come up with in terms of suggested improvements. If you decide that you want to totally revamp your bathroom, you'll also need to think about whether you want to keep the existing layout and replace any fixtures and fittings in the same configuration. What might have once worked, may no longer.

Accessorise!

If your budget is limited add some simple touches to make your bathroom more enjoyable and inviting:-

*   Add some scented candles to your bathroom and light them when you take a bath – with a well-deserved glass of wine you can make bath-time a real treat!

*   If you've a free shelf in the bathroom, add a bowl of fragrant pot-pourri or some well-chosen fabric flowers.

*   Place some favourite photos or artwork on the walls in your bathroom.

*   Purchase a luxurious-looking shower curtain, matching the feel of the bathroom, to give your bathroom an instant lift.

*   Change the blinds or curtains in your bathroom – or simply take them down and give them a wash. You'll be surprised at what a difference it makes.

*   Add a comfortable chair or storage box with a comfortable seated lid. This can multi-function as a welcome sit down, somewhere to paint your toe-nails, a place for your children to sit and dry themselves or a way to keep your clothes off the floor!

*   Decorative mirrors will add light and a more beauty to the bathroom. You could even make an antique or ornate mirror a focal point in the bathroom, by placing it above the sink and with a spotlight highlighting it.

*   Change old accessories for brand new ones, such as toilet roll holders, towel rails, light switches/pulls, taps and toothbrush holders. Simple but effective.

*   If you've small children, stencil the wall around the bath with characters or pictures that they'll enjoy. Alternatively you can buy fun stickers that stick on the bottom of the bath, such as fish, starfish, etc – and they're removable too. Your kids will love them!

Cladding

Cladding is a waterproof form of wall paneling that is becoming more and more popular, as an alternative to ceramic tiles. It's also a welcome departure from mould-prone grout because of the way in which cladding is slotted into place.

An attractive looking paneling, cladding can be used around baths, showers and in wet rooms. Cladding is available in a range of different effects, such as marble, tile, woodgrain, mosaic, laminate and solid wood effects.

Cladding is easily cleaned and also provides a little extra insulation for walls. If you've never used cladding before it's a good idea to do your research into the different types in order to decide whether it's right for you.

Flooring

As well as being aesthetically pleasing, your bathroom floor needs to be pretty resilient. Needing to stand up to lots of people-traffic, plenty of water (just have kids!), product spills, potty-training accidents, dropped make-up, bleach and cleaning products, talcum powder, etc… your flooring needs to have the wipe-ability factor never mind anything else! Ultimately, if you choose the right flooring for your bathroom, you can create a really beautiful space, one that looks brighter, larger and more inviting.

Ceramic & Porcelain Tiles

Give your bathroom floor a real treat and go for the beauty and resilience of ceramic or porcelain tiles. There are literally hundreds of different styles and colours, so you'll be sure to find something that's perfect for your bathroom needs. When choosing your tiles take into consideration the size of your bathroom and the type of traffic that goes through it. Take some advice if you're not sure – you'll most probably be intending for the floor to be there long-term, so making the right choice is vital.

Vinyl Floors

If your budget is a little on the stretched side then expensive flooring doesn't need to be at the top of your list. If you're concentrating on improving your bathroom at eye-level, flooring can be looked at from a more affordable perspective. Vinyl flooring comes in a sheet or square format, with an extensive range of textures, styles and colours. A versatile and easy to clean option, the wide range of varieties will make it easy for you to match to your bathroom. It's worth remembering that vinyl flooring in sheet form will provide better waterproofing than tiles; by design.

Cork Tiles

Once a very popular sight, cork tiles are also an option for your bathroom floor. Despite their recent decline in popularity they provide flooring positives, such as being warmer and softer under foot than tiles or vinyl – they also provide a certain amount of insulation. Practically, they're water resistant, so will withstand spills and water soaked footprints. So, if you're after a warmer, more natural feel to your flooring then cork tiles could be the improvement that you're looking for.

Freshen Up The Walls & Ceiling

Give your bathroom an instant lift by painting it! You can opt for a more daring colour, or just give it a new coat of the same colour. Either way you'll revitalise the look and energy of the room. If you're changing the colour, think about what you want to achieve, e.g. do you want to lighten up your bathroom or go for a warmer, more comfortable look. Maybe try a feature wall of a deeper, bolder colour, contrasted by lighter, calmer colours. Don't forget to go for kitchen/bathroom paint so that it's waterproof. Just remember that how you decorate your walls will have a bigger impact on your bathroom than the furniture you use, so think carefully about your choices.

Knock Through

If your bathroom and toilet are located in separate rooms, adjacent to each other – it might well be worth your while knocking through and making one bigger room. It might sound like an upheaval, but you it will give you much more room to play with in terms of free floor/wall space and design options.

Mirror, Mirror...

Your bathroom will be the place where family members will shave, wash, cleanse, floss, etc – so a good quality mirror is a must. A magnified mirror is great for shaving and other close-up needs, but it's also worth having an illuminated mirror to give you an even clearer view of what you're doing. Illuminated mirrors are particularly helpful for applying make-up on dark mornings. Dim lighting can make it look like you've not got much make-up on, so you may end up applying more than you need; finding out to your horror mid-morning that you've actually applied a rather convincing Drag-Queen look!

On The Tiles!

If your bathroom tiles are a little tired looking or on the old fashioned side, then maybe changing them is an option that you can consider. Shop around and find something that inspires you. You'll find an extensive amount of choice when it comes to style, texture and colour; and there'll be plenty of help out there if you need a little advice and direction.

On the other hand, if replacing your bathroom tiles isn't an option at the moment, then it's quite possible that the tiles in your bathroom would be much improved by just freshening them up with a new colour. Simply buy some tile paint, don your painting gear and breathe some new life into them!

Whether you're painting or replacing you tiles, if your bathroom lacks a bit of light then go for a lighter/brighter colour – you'll be surprised at how much you'll open up the space by simply opening up your colour palette.

Privacy Screen

If you've the room in your bathroom, think about adding a privacy screen which can be used to get some much needed privacy, (especially if you've got children who insist on following you everywhere!) – and you can also double it up to hide aspects of your bathroom that you don't want anyone to see, e.g. cleaning products.

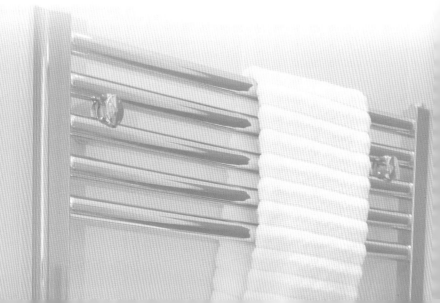

Remodelling Your Bathroom

If you're thinking about having your bathroom remodelled, then you'll need to have a good handle on the practicalities, as well as the design aesthetics of such a project. If your budget plays a big part in your plans then succinct planning will be essential. When thinking about repositioning your bathroom and replacing an old bathroom suite you'll need to begin by considering some of the following issues:-

*   When planning your ideal bathroom, how are you going to best utilise the 'useable' space? How will you minimise areas of 'dead' space?

*   What practical pitfalls are there? e.g. drainage, plumbing etc.

*   Do you need new lighting to be incorporated in with your plans?

*   Does the style of bathroom suite that you want suit your property?

*   Does the style of bathroom suite you want suit the size and feel of your bathroom?

*   Do your plans take account of the necessary storage needed?

*   How do your plans realistically fit in with your budget?

*   Do you have a contingency amount of money to cover any problems? If so, is this realistic?

One way to discern what is right for you is to utilise the services of bathroom suppliers and their design software, which is available in most outfitters.

All you need to do is take the dimensions of your bathroom, pick some bathroom suite styles that you like and the staff will assist you in building your ideal bathroom – giving you a 3D perspective of how it will look in reality. However, before you commit to a purchase, ensure that your supplier has taken exact measurements – just to rule out any measuring errors.

Showers

If you've only ever had a bath in your home, then maybe you're interested in installing a shower as part of your home-improvement kick. If so, there are a myriad of different styles and types available. If you're not sure what would be most suitable, rather then bamboozle yourself by looking on the Internet at all the different possibilities, it's probably better to go down to a number of different showrooms and take a look in-person. You'll be able to get some expert advice and get a more realistic sense of the costs involved. If a fair amount of your bathroom space is taken up by a bath and you could do with the extra room, then why not consider replacing the bath with a power-shower? This won't be possible in a house with small children or babies, but if this isn't an issue then installing a shower stall in place of a bath will create more available space in your bathroom.

Space Savers

The bathroom can be a real challenge in terms of storage and space. With the masses of products and toiletries that can overwhelm every surface, versatility will be key in making great home-improvements. Here are a few tips to get you started:-

Clear Out!

Clear out any old products or unused items from surfaces, drawers and shelves. If you've had them there, unused, for any longer than six months you've managed without them thus far – so be brutal and get rid!

Baskets

To help avoid constantly cluttered surfaces in your bathroom, designate a basket to each household member for non-shared toiletry items and products.

The baskets can either be kept in each person's bedroom space or stored within available bathroom cabinet space, if the baskets will fit inside.

Not only will this save on counter space, but it will reduce the amount of time that family members spend looking for misplaced items... not to mention putting a stop to unauthorised-product-borrowing!

Slim-Line Units
Make the most of your storage space by investing in freestanding, slim-line storage units; preferably with built-in shelves and/or deep drawers. Properly positioned they will save floor space and make an attractive storage solution.

Wall Space
Make use of your wall space by erecting shelving or a medicine-style cabinet to house daily, shared toiletry, cleansing and bathing products.

Children's Bath Toys
Children's toys can make bathrooms look pretty cluttered, not to mention the time it takes to get them out of the bath before you can actually get into your own bath! Look into purchasing either a plastic storage container to store them in, or a hammock-like storage net with suction pads that stick to the side of the bath. These will not only effectively store the toys but they'll also allow for proper drainage and drying time.

Hooks
If you've a large family, then the amount of towels, dressing gowns, flannels, etc can create a real mess in your bathroom. Over-door or wall hooks are great space savers and don't take up nearly as much room as towel racks. For an extra sense of order, it's worth identifying an individual hook for each family member. For children, remember to make sure that they can reach their hooks!

Double-Up
If your bathroom is spatially challenged, don't despair! Look out for items that you will double-up in terms of their functionality - such as a medicine-style cabinet with mirrored doors, a solid wooden laundry/linen box with a padded seat, a sink housed within a storage unit, etc.

Speed-Up Mornings!

If you've a busy household with lots of children to ferry through the bathroom, then installing two sinks in your bathroom will help to speed up those fraught school mornings!

Ventilation

A simple way to improve your bathroom is to ensure that it is well ventilated. Excessive moisture in your bathroom can lift wallpaper, damage paint and cause damp, mould patches which can be a nightmare to get rid of.

Wall Tiles

If you're tiling your bathroom floor as part of your home improvement plans, you might also want to make cleaning and maintaining your bathroom even easier, by opting to cover your walls with tiles too. It will uniform your décor and give your bathroom a sleek, finished look.

However, if your budget won't stretch that far or you don't like the idea of your whole bathroom being tiled, perhaps think about tiling the splash-back area behind your sink and/or surrounding your bath, or perhaps tiling the area in which you stand to have a shower.

Water Flow

Is the flow of water into your bathroom a little on the limp side? Is your power-shower not fulfilling its destiny? If so, then your water pressure could well be the problem. A water pump may be the answer, but unless you've plumbing know-how, then get a professional opinion. Unless you have a recommendation from a trusted source, get a few separate opinions and quotes.

Weight Checks

If your improvements involve any radical changes in terms of adding extra weight to your bathroom - such as a cast-iron bath to give it a period-feel – make sure that you check first whether the floor will take the weight; remembering that, that will include the weight of the bath filled with water. You don't want any nasty surprises or to pose any danger to the rest of your household.

New Additions

New Additions

New Additions & The Child-Friendly Home

It wasn't so long ago, in the 40's and 50's that the home had separate domains for mum, dad and children – but we no longer subscribe to this point of view and our homes are now generally communal to all family members and not subject to adult/child segregation. This being the case, we need our homes to be evermore versatile. A home with no children is a whole different affair to a home with children in – especially small children and babies! If you've new additions to your household, then you'll know that it's something akin to a whirlwind that takes over your life and suddenly your home is fraught with areas of the home that are no longer appropriate for small fingers and feet.

So how do we make the communal areas of our home into something that will suit the wonderful chaos, curiosity and liveliness of children, but that will still be an adult haven when we need it? Flexibility is key - allowing these areas of the home to be switched around and changed with the minimum amount of stress and fuss. For instance, the lounge should be comfortable and cosy enough for all the family to chill-out and relax of an evening or weekend – and stylish and chic enough for an evening of adult entertaining.

Beginnings – Childproofing

The first natural steps are for you to childproof your home as soon as your babies are on the move, from approximately six months. Childproofing your home will include :-

*   Cover electrical points and outlets

*   Place child-safety locks on cabinets, cupboards and drawers

*   Install stair gates and window guards

*   Move household cleaners, medicines and other chemicals out of reach and in a locked cabinet

*   Remove small items, which present choking hazards out of the way

*   Cover sharp corners with soft, protective or plastic covers

*   Either tack rugs down or affix non-slip backing to them

*   Erect secure fireguards

*   Buy cooker/stove guards

*   Remove breakables from accessible points around your home

*   Tie curtain and blind cords well out of reach

*   Enclose ponds, water features or swimming pools with a fence – either that or fill them in or remove them.

*   Keep doors that lead into utility rooms or garages permanently locked.

For more comprehensive guidance about child safety consult qualified individuals and organisations, such as www.homesafetycouncil.org or www.whoopschildsafety.co.uk.

New Additions

Toddlers and Beyond...

Once your children are past the baby stage, it's equally as important to keep the home safe, but at the same time you can take steps to it having more of a communal and inclusive family feel.

Face Facts

Firstly, let's face it – children won't be and shouldn't be concerning themselves with making sure that your beige/cream lounge-paradise stays that way! Teaching them to respect property is one thing, but making them overly conscious of just sitting down on the sofa is another thing altogether. Child-friendly means more than just safety, it means being just that – friendly! Equally, as a parent you want to enjoy your children being young, they all but canter through childhood so you don't want to miss it; and being uptight about your furnishings is not conducive to taking pleasure in watching them grow and learn. A more relaxed and laidback parent is a certainly a happier one! Honestly!

Kitchen & Dining Area

Comfy Seating

If your space allows, it's lovely to have a safe area of the kitchen where your children can sit in comfort – be it beanbags, two-seater sofas or some other comfy-seat option. That way they can sit and chat to you whilst you're busy in the kitchen, giving both you and your children time together that you wouldn't otherwise have. In fact, it's likely it'll attract more members of your household into the kitchen, encouraging more family time together – maybe even teenagers too!

Crockery

When there are children around the amount of crockery you get through can be quite alarming at times! So, to stop you from opening your cupboards to bare boards, it's a good idea to stock-up with a generous selection of crockery.

It doesn't have to cost a fortune; just basic ranges from your local supermarket will make do – which will also make inevitable breakages easier to bear.

Décor

The décor for your kitchen needs to tread a precarious line between being warm and cosy for your children; stylish and elegant for adult entertaining; and a little bit on the modern/funky side for your teenagers. Not much to ask then!

With so many needs to consider, it's a good idea to paint a reasonably neutral canvas with regards to your walls, floors, tops and cabinets – making a concerted effort with your accessories to accommodate the needs of all the different ages within the house.

For instance, you could have a zone in the kitchen which has a brightly coloured wall, where there are photos, prized homemade art & craft work and fun lights for the younger members of the household; contrasted with another area which houses stylish and classic shapes and textures, with elegant accessories for grown-up dinner parties.

Dinner Parties

Ideally, children will be in bed in time for adult dinner parties – but then, we don't live in an ideal world. If you've younger children who play-up on these occasions, you have two choices – you either don't have dinner parties or you endure continual shouts for mummy/daddy during your meal, bringing on feelings of excruciating embarrassment and awful guilt. Either option isn't exactly attractive. So, instead of battling the impossible, then consider a compromise by placing a little table and chairs in the dining area and allowing them to have a little bit of 'dinner', alongside you and your guests for the first course (which could simply be crudités); after which, they are allowed to say goodnight before being taken up to bed. Children can't stand feeling like they're missing out, so if you're stuck in this dilemma, it'll give them a sense of having been involved and any curiosity about your guests will be satisfied. Any screaming after that can be guilt free!

NB. It's polite to run this idea past your prospective guests to give them the opportunity to accept or decline your invitation. Not everyone will understand!

Dishwasher

If you don't already have one – get one! Unless you want to spend your life at the sink, of course!

Flooring

Above any other consideration, your family kitchen floor will need to be robust! Needing to stand up to lots of foot-traffic, food spills, dropped cutlery and cooking utensils, children playing games, scooters, tricycles, etc – your flooring will go through some punishing times, so choose with your individual household in mind.

Kitchen Design

If you're thinking of re-designing your kitchen, then free-flowing zones are going to be an important consideration to make a child-friendly room. Children enjoy space and in a kitchen environment, it's safer for you and your children if you have more free-flowing space. Don't be afraid to move away from the set idea of traditionally styled kitchens, such as L-shaped or U-shaped designs. A generous amount of floor place will be good for adult gatherings, as well as smaller children's parties.

Kitchen Tables

When picking a kitchen table, you'll need to think not just about mealtimes but the scores of other uses you'll need it for… arts and crafts, baking, an impromptu drum (using spoons and other cutlery), science experiments, homework… even possibly a climbing frame. So a robust, easy to clean and sturdy table is a must. If you want something that will be suitable for evenings and adult entertaining too, then it's probably worth covering your table with a thick, plastic covering, (available from most hardware and kitchenware outlets), for when your little darlings are going to be sat at the table eating; or trying to annihilate it by any means possible!

Step Stools

Step stools wonderful way to encourage your child to feel a bit more independent. Helping them to reach into the sink to wash their hands, reach a cupboard or pass something to mummy or daddy. Naturally, step stools should be sturdy and should be used with very small children ONLY when an adult is present. If you have a step stool in your kitchen, make sure that any dangerous items are placed well back, locked away or in a cupboard that they still can't reach.

Unit Space

When your children are little and spend time playing at the kitchen table, make room in your kitchen units for all their play-needs – such as paints, pencils, paper, crafts, apron, books, toys, board games, favourite CDs, etc. Choosing a unit in a safe and accessible place is also a good idea, so that children can help themselves. Place a fun sticker that they'll recognise on the front, so that they know that that's where their play-things are.

Lounge

Add Child-Friendly Accessories

Keeping your minimalist-style lounge is your perogative, of course – but why not personalise it a little more and add a few accessories that will be pleasing to your children… jewelled cushions, twinkling chandeliers, luxuriously textured throws and cushions, a fluffy deep-pile rug, fairy-lights sitting in a tall vase, a brightly coloured wall canvas, etc… it will bring a more child-friendly, homely feel to your lounge and if you want to transform your room back for adult entertaining, then you can move the accessories to another room.

Be Flexible

Children need boundaries to feel safe and know what's expected of them, so family rules which state that there should be no sticky-buns on the sofa or no coca-cola drinking over the lounge rug may be non-negotiable. However, don't make your lounge area so rigid that your children can't move – they just won't want to sit in it. So some flexibility will encourage them in and make your lounge feel child-friendly. For instance, if it's the only place that your five-year old son can really spread out his toy soldiers and create a proper battleground, with hidey-holes and lookout towers, (cleverly made out of books, of course) – then what's the harm? If you can give them the space and time, they'll have a great time – and as long as you teach them to put everything away and to clear up after themselves, you'll be giving them a real sense of freedom and being a valued part of the household.

Of course, it doesn't have to be as elaborate as that, it can be something as simple as having a low-set table in the lounge area where your youngsters can do their favourite jigsaws, or play a game of cards.

Book Shelving

Encourage a love of books by making them accessible to all of your children, even toddlers and babies. Age appropriate books can be placed on different levels on a bookcase, with hard-paged books for babies and toddlers on the bottom – gradually grading upwards in age, little by little. If you're worried about books being ruined, then buy them from secondhand book or charity shops. That way you won't get upset when Paddington Bear ends up being fed a soggy biscuit.

Breakables

Until your children are old enough, there's not much point in you and them being stressed about treasured or expensive items in your lounge that are breakable. So, until they're old to appreciate ornate objects from a distance, then move them out.

Family Photos & Memorabilia

Create a wonderfully personal, cosy family atmosphere by adding an array of family photos and memorabilia. It could be an array of personal treasures, such as sea-shells found by your two year old at the seaside, a pressing of a flower that your daughter picked for you when she was on her way from school, a black and white print of your cheeky twins on their birthday, grandma and granddad's 60th anniversary… whatever makes all of you happy. Change the items every now and again, storing the older items in a special box and laying out new ones. Involve your children in deciding what items go where, they'll love the feeling of being included.

New Additions

Flooring

Children just seem to be drawn to floor level...whether it's laying face down asleep, rolling around on the floor creating new and undiscovered gymnastic moves, crayoning abstract pictures that Picasso would have been proud of, coaxing the dog to eat their unwanted lunch or laying flat on their backs admiring the Artex ceiling...for hours.

Whatever their movements, small children will love soft floorings. So, ideally you should either go for 100% wool carpeting, making it easier to clean or wooden flooring, covered by inexpensive but comfortable rugs. Darker coloured rugs are more of a sensible option in terms of hiding stains.

Side Tables

Although spills are inevitable, adding side tables to the side of each chair will reduce the potential for accidents.

Storage

Storage is a must-have in a family lounge; toys, books, DVDs, CDs, photo albums, board games, books... the list goes on. Whether you opt for an

open wall unit, closed cabinets or labeled boxes; involve your children in clear-up time at the end of the day. You can even make a game of it, racing them to see who can get the most put away in the shortest time.

Television & Console Games

If your television is going to be the centre point of interest in your family lounge, it's no good being coy about it and pretending that it doesn't matter to your non-television-viewing friends – stand up and be proud in your television placement! These days there are so many family games that can be played together on varying games console mediums – bowling, tennis, racing, boxing and even fitness regimes!

Place your television at its optimum viewing point in the room and arrange the furniture around it. Just remember that balance is everything and you control how much screen entertainment is allowed in your household.

Versatile Seating

Most children LOVE floor cushions, beanbags or seating cubes, so why not invest in some for your lounge area? They can be bought fairly cheaply and if you don't want them clogging-up your lounge when you have company or you just want some adult-time, then they can be moved out of the way and doubled up as seating for your children's rooms.

Washable is Best!

Just have children…will have spills. Fact. There is no such thing as a cup that doesn't leak, or a child that doesn't drop a full cup of blackcurrant juice! Protect any precious furniture, carpets and other materials that you want to keep safe with washable covers, throws, rugs, blankets, etc. Wooden floors can feel a little cold to some, but they're a God-send when your five year old has just dropped his bowl of Co-co Pops all over floor. Bless…

When it comes to walls, go washable…every time! Not everyone is keen on the sheen that washable paint gives, but it's a temporary measure until you're confident that the number of sticky-mucky-finger moments have dissipated enough. Either that or be prepared to be painting every few months!

New Additions

Bathroom Location

If you have small children, it's best to have their bedrooms on the same floor as the bathroom, so that nighttime toilet visits are easier and you don't have to worry about them negotiating staircases whilst they're sleepy...or you being woken up by little ones needing a pee!

Bathroom Space

If you've only one small bathroom for a large family, consider either moving it or knocking through to an adjacent room. For example, if your bathroom and toilet are located next to each other – it might well be worth your while knocking through and making one bigger room. It might sound like an upheaval, but it would give you much more room to play with in terms of free floor/wall space and design options. If you have enough room in your existing bathroom, think about adding an additional shower stall – so that more than one person at a time can take a shower. Either that, or convert a small box room, utility room or dead space at the end of a hallway or landing, into a small shower room and toilet. It'll save queues at busy times and little crossed legs!

Bath Toys

Children's toys can make bathrooms look pretty cluttered, not to mention the time it takes to get them out of the bath before you can actually get into your own bath! Look into purchasing either a plastic storage container to store them in, or a hammock-like storage net with suction pads that stick to the side of the bath. These will not only effectively store the toys but they'll also allow for proper drainage and drying time.

Bigger Bath!

Having a bigger bath will allow you to bath younger siblings together, with room for them to play and splash around too.

And of course, what a wonderful way for you to recline and take a long, luxurious bath too!

Chairs

Add a comfortable chair, a two-seater sofa (with washable cover) or storage box with a comfortable seated lid. Any of these seating options can multi-function as a place for your children to sit and undress, dry themselves or get dressed again – as well as keeping their clothes off the floor! Or they may just want to come in, sit down and read you their favourite story whilst you're taking a dip! As the saying goes, no peace for the wicked. Or parents.

Décor

If your children have a separate bath or shower room, then make it bright and fun. Funky coloured paint, glittery tiles or colourful mosaics, framed pictures of cartoon characters or other favourites, colourful accessories, bright fluffy towels and lots of bubble bath!

Flooring

As well as being aesthetically pleasing, your family bathroom floor needs to be pretty resilient. Needing to stand up to lots of splashing water, spills, potty-training accidents, talcum powder, toothpaste dribbles, etc - your flooring needs to have the wipe-ability factor never mind anything else! Go for something that is robust, but safe – such as wood, stone, rubber or the ever-popular lino.

Hooks & Towel Racks

If you've a large family you'll know that the amount of towels, dressing gowns, flannels, etc can create a real mess in your bathroom! Over-door or wall hooks are great space savers. For an extra bit of order, it's worth identifying an individual hook for each family member. For children, remember to make sure that they can reach their hooks. If hooks aren't enough, then think about a heated towel rack, which will dry towels as well as keeping them off the floor!

Medicines

Medicines shouldn't be kept in the bathroom whether you have children or not, due to temperature storage requirements – but a lot of people do. If you have children, take them out of the bathroom and lock them away somewhere where children can't reach them.

Speed-Up Mornings!

If you've a busy household with lots of children to ferry through the bathroom, then installing two sinks in your bathroom will help to speed up those fraught school mornings. Although be prepared for the inevitable sibling elbowing if your sinks are set together.

Stencils & Stickers

If you've small children, stencil the wall around the bath with characters or pictures that they'll enjoy. Alternatively you can buy fun stickers that stick on the bottom of the bath, such as fish, starfish, etc – and they're removable too. Your kids will love them!

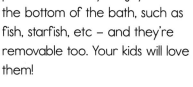

Stools

If you have very little ones who can't reach the toilet, sink, etc – provide a sturdy stool for them to stand on.

Garden

Garden

Improve Your Garden

Is your garden a little lack-lustre? Are your plants and flowers floundering or just not growing at all? Or is your garden akin to a 'concrete jungle', with the only thriving plant-life being in the shape of weeds infiltrating the paving slabs? If so, then you might be either feeling a tad frustrated that your efforts seem to be in vain, or that you don't have an environment within which you can create any type of garden.

If, like most of us, you're not in a position to employ the services of a top-notch landscape gardener, or even just your neighbourhood gardener – don't despair because improving your garden is not as hard as you think. So, whether you decide to make a brand new start on your existing garden, or whether you just want to add some colourful floral pots and tasteful features to your garden, improving it to your liking will make the world of difference.

Out with the Old!
Home and garden improvement is a good time to start afresh, so go out into your garden and with fresh eyes, really look it – almost as though it doesn't belong to you. What are the obvious eyesores? Rusting or warping garden chairs? One of your children's old bikes? A pile of old fence panels? Bin bags? Broken garden pots? A rotting trellis? A splitting, (to the point of bursting), compost bin? Whatever eyesores exist, or items that are no longer a part of your life now – get them moved. Take them to the tip, recycle them, give them to charity... whatever it takes.

The Five Senses
To really get the most out of improving your garden, think about what you want from it in terms of sight, sounds, smells, touch and even taste! Think about the shapes, colours, textures, scents and sights you might want to create for yourself. Talk as a family and maybe agree on areas that will incorporate certain aspects, reflecting each other's individual tastes. Ideas you could incorporate are; home-grown fruits and vegetables, wonderfully colourful and exotic plants and flowers, a fragrant herb garden, the sound of running water, the encouragement of wildlife, creating a play area, cultivating a sprawling lawn, making a place to sip

wine under archways and pergolas with gently aromatic and romantic blooms or a tranquil haven where you can sit and read or listen to bird song, having fragrant wisteria greeting you at the entrance to your house, stunning garden lights or creating an ornate centrepiece. Your choices are endless and up to you… cost, space and time allowing.

Make a Plan!

So you don't have a qualification in landscape garden… so what? There is no great mystery to improving your garden, so don't be intimidated by the legions of gardening or home-improvement programmes that would have you believe that you need a team of experts to make your garden into a colourful, fragrant and visual delight! All you need is a vision of what you would like your garden to look like, (starting with simple steps if you're a bit of a novice), basic knowledge to start you off and the willingness to learn and work hard at cultivating your new creation! It's an idea to make a scaled sketch of your garden, working out what you'd like where – and making sure that your ideas can become reality, however simple or complex.

Location, Location, Location!

Before you start planting or rearranging your garden in a fit of enthusiasm, think carefully about the position of your garden in relation to other factors, such as; the direction of the sun, other plants, areas of your garden that are prone to becoming waterlogged, neighbours trees, etc. For example, which part of the garden does the sun shine in all day? Where are the shady parts? Are there trees overhanging your garden? Where are the most exposed parts of your garden? Which parts of the garden could do with livening up? Where are the quietest spots in the garden? Where would the children be best playing in terms of space and safety?

Wildlife

Whatever your aesthetic preferences are for your garden, if you're a wildlife lover, take time to consider what you'd like to attract to your garden… butterflies, birds, squirrels, ladybirds and other friendly insects, bumble bees, frogs, dragonflies, hedgehogs… be mindful that the choices you make within your garden will either encourage or discourage differing types of wildlife.

Test Your Soil

Do your homework and get to know the quality of the soil in your garden. Your local garden centre will sell pH test kits, so that you can test your soil, and where appropriate get advice on how to improve the quality of your soil and what plants and flowers will thrive best in it.

Planting Seeds

It may be a taboo subject for some members of the male sex, but reading instructions is an absolute must when buying seed packets! You will need to know whether they are best sown straight into the ground, in pots or trays, how often they need watering, whether they need pre-soaking, what sort of soil they need, etc.

Plant Care

If you're investing in new plants, do your homework on how to care for them on an on-going process, as their needs will change as they begin to grow and bloom. The levels of space, warmth, watering, air, sunlight and shade will differ from plant to plant. That way you'll get the maximum enjoyment from your plants and you'll really reap the rewards from all your care and hard work. Knowing what care your plants will need should be a big part of deciding which plants to have in your garden. If you've time on your hands, the world's your oyster – but if not, you'll want to make sure that you choose plants that are not too high maintenance and that you have the time and inclination to care for them.

Watering

How much watering will depend on the type of plants you have in your garden. But what is always key to remember is that when watering your plants, the most effective method is to water as near to the roots as possible - giving them a quick sprinkle over the top won't suffice and you'll soon see them flounder.

Garden

Compost

Don't skimp on good compost if you're planting new plants or flowers – and do your homework into which types of compost will suit which plants. If you're planting in pots, do not use soil from your garden as this may well come contaminated with any pests or diseases existing in the soil; and your newly planted plants will not have enough nutrients to achieve their full potential and give you gorgeous and plentiful blooms. If you've the room and inclination, buy a home composting bin and utilise raw materials from your garden and kitchen. If you take this route, make sure that you read up on what you should and shouldn't add to your compost heap.

Walls & Other Structures

You might want to give your whole garden a facelift, which might involve some quite radical plans in terms of walls and other permanent structures – but the best advice is to create the style of garden that you would like, in terms of planting and style, (keeping in mind other changes you may want to make), and live with them for a while – allowing yourself to get used to the look of your garden. The last thing you want is to spend time and money building structures, which after a few months you decide that you don't like.

Water Features

Water features can add a real sense of calm and tranquility to a garden. If you'd like to make your garden a more tranquil place, a water feature just might be a welcome improvement for you. If you've not had one before, it's an idea to start off thinking 'small' to see how you get on, (i.e. you don't have to have a mini-lake in your back garden!). It's also worth considering how near you are to your neighbours, as the bigger the feature, the louder the running water.

Create the Illusion of Space

Even if you have a small space to work with, fashion the impression of more space by creating different levels, or by utilising existing peaks and troughs in your garden area. For instance, raise-up an area using decking and create a patio area; or create a rockery on a slope, spattered with a diversity of hardy plants and beautiful blooms. Even different sized pots, planted with a range of flowers and plants can create the illusion of differing levels within a flat or small area.

Make it Interesting

If your garden space is a little on the predictable side, (in your own opinion, of course!), with a patch of grass surrounded by borders - engage your imagination and think intriguing, think alluring… make your garden a welcoming and interesting place that will appeal not only to you, but to your family, friends and even your neighbours! Add little winding pathways, a decorative fence, curved flowerbeds, a trellis with abundant climbers, fill a wheelbarrow with trailing plants and flowers, create a seating area tucked away under a tree or in a sunny corner, erect a pergola, add an ornate birdbath or a sundial, adorn the borders with night lanterns… or simply add some outside lighting for summer evenings. There are a wide range of possibilities for you to consider – none of which have to cost you the earth, just a little creativity and a bit of graft!

Ornamental Grasses

As an alternative to shrubs and higher maintenance flowerbeds, ornamental grasses are an attractive addition to your garden's borders and boundaries. The taller varieties can also be a welcome addition of privacy to your garden.

Tackle Garden Critters & Diseases!

If your garden is under attack from unwanted pests and diseases, then it's highly probable that any would-be glorious blooms and plants will be at best, struggling – or worse, on their last legs. Hardly a reason for you to want to sit and relax in your garden; or a welcoming sight as the setting for your home. A large part of your plants' health and wellbeing will be dependant on good soil and fertiliser in the right amounts, as well as regular watering and nutrients. If any of these are neglected then your plants can soon begin to suffer, leaving them open to disease and pests, which will quickly spread due to the weakened state of your plants. As well as keeping optimum conditions for your plants to thrive, it's important to keep a sharp eye out for pests and any diseases and deal with them before they have taken a good hold. The best form of defence, of course is attack and there are plenty of products available to protect your plants and eradicate destructive pests and diseases, including some that are environmentally friendly, such as soap sprays and derris. However, some will be harmful to the useful insects in your garden and others may not be pet-friendly – so check labels and instructions carefully before purchasing.

Herb Garden

If you're keen to devote some of your garden improvements to home-grown produce, herbs are a fabulous way to flex your kitchen-garden muscles! Herbs are great as you can pretty much have them anywhere in your garden, be it in a border, a mixed bed of plants, a hanging basket or container.

As long as you read up what each herbs will need in terms of conditions and care, e.g. moisture, light, shade, drainage, etc; then you have a wide range of options. Try herbs such as parsley, mint, rosemary, chives, coriander, basil and dill. There's certainly nothing like the fragrance of fresh herbs wafting through your kitchen door and being able to go out and snip them on demand!

Container Gardening

Not having a 'garden' in the traditional sense is not a deterrent from being able to grow beautiful displays of flowers, trees and even vegetables – even if you have just a small space like a patio, balcony, porch, etc. So if you are struggling for space, have poor quality soil, suffering from a lack of light or have little time to maintain a full sized garden, container gardening might just be the answer you're looking for! And for existing gardens, needing that something a little extra, container gardening can add an array of different shapes, colours, fragrances and stunning architecture to any garden... large or small.

You can have potted plants all year round, as long as the containers and plants are suitable for the season. Their versatility means that their contents can be changed with the seasons; and if they are not too heavy, they can be moved around for different groupings or singled out for a solo display, giving you a delightful display and a range of choices throughout the seasons!

NB. When you are choosing your containers always make sure that they have drainage holes, just like the regular plant pots. If they don't, the roots of the plants can become diseased and rot as the soil will be sour, the leaves will turn yellow and growth can be retarded.

Hanging Baskets

Hanging baskets can quickly brighten up the dullest doorway and add a welcome sparkle to any bare patio or porch – or just add a bit of 'oomph' to an already flowering garden. If you opt for these beautiful floral additions, be aware that they are quite labour intensive, needing lots of water, feeding and dead-heading in order to keep up that luscious full appearance, which a well planted basket can yield.

Banish Weeds

If your garden has been taken over by these ever-growing nuisances, then the chances are that your garden is not a place that you spend much time in! But your garden could be the world of a different place without them.

Annoyingly resilient, fast-growing and pretty much always a pain! But by giving your garden enough care and attention, they don't have to ruin your home and garden improvement dreams.

Like plants and flowers, weeds are both annual and perennial. Annuals can pretty much be easily dealt with by either pulling them out of damp soil, or digging them up and chopping them with a hoe. However, perennials will take a little more work and will need digging up by the root and removing every trace.

Get some advice from your local garden centre for the best products to suit your garden environment.

Make it a haven for you, your family and friends and not for these annoying intruders!

Winter Wonderland

Your garden doesn't have to be a source of neglect and floral disappointment during the winter months. The trusty evergreen will always give your garden that beautiful deep green splendour, which looks even more stunning when covered by the winter frosts. And pruning and clipping your trees and bushes will make sure that they never lose their shape. But winter gardening doesn't have to mean the absence of flowers and colour; there are a surprising amount of blooms that will survive the hard bite of winter and will give you pleasure from the warmth of your living rooms.

To get the optimum enjoyment, plant winter flowers near to the house, along pathways and in borders. Try Caillcarpa Bodinieri with their beautifully vibrant berries, Chimonanthus praecox Luteus with blooming yellow flowers on wintery stems and Viburnum x bodnantense flowering an unseasonal, but beautiful pink blossom. And of course, not forgetting the beautiful sight of snowdrops in January/February – bringing a reminder that spring is just around the corner.

If you've little or no garden area to work with, erect a well-positioned trellis or archway and create a winter centrepiece for your garden - even if it's one entwined with beautiful outside lighting. It'll make the world of difference when the nights draw in and you can look outside your window to a garden lit-up with sparkling lights.

Patio Facelift

Is your concrete patio area looking a little sad and worn? If so, try a quick improvement by laying some fresh and attractive looking flagstone slabs – to overlay and cover the old area. Prevent weeds from infiltrating your brick or stone patio area by sprinkling rock salt over the area in spring. The salt will soak into the ground area in between and kill off any weeds that would be ready to make their appearance during growing season.

Create a Focal Point

To easily create a focal point in your garden, without a great deal of effort, choose an appropriately sized statue and place it in your chosen position. Statuettes such as Buddhas, Easter Island heads, fairies, dragons and cherubs are often popular.